CHAPPELL ROAN

CHAPPELL ROAN

A VIBRANT JOURNEY THROUGH THE CAREER AND INFLUENCE OF THE INDIE-POP SUPERSTAR

Harbert Day

EPIC INK

Contents

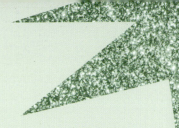

Prologue: Chappell on Stage	7
Track 1: A Girl Named Kayleigh	13
Track 2: Part-Time Pop Star	41
Track 3: The Inclusive Queen	83
Track 4: Stage Princess	119
Track 5: Chappell the Star	159
Epilogue: The Next Tracklist	191
Discography	197
Awards and Nominations	198
Sources	200
Photo Credits	204
Acknowledgments	206
About the Author	207

PREVIOUS
Chappell's costumes usually include elaborate fingernail designs. Her arriving outfit for the 2024 MTV Video Music Awards was no exception.

OPPOSITE
Chappell attends Netflix's LA premiere for "Olivia Rodrigo: GUTS World Tour" on October 25, 2024.

Prologue: Chappell on Stage

When "Good Luck, Babe!" begins, Chappell Roan is standing behind a large gate that looks like it's made of iron. There's some kind of dimly lit house behind her—a castle, maybe, with torches visible just behind the spotlight illuminating her red hair. It's tied in two braids, and is more efficient-seeming than childlike, because she's also wearing a full suit of chainmail armor. In her hands is a bow, holding an arrow on fire. The doors open, and she slowly strides between two lines of six soldiers, dancers who turn out to have an elaborate routine worked out that incorporates their swords.

She turns, and the audience can see that Chappell's costume is (as usual) what *The Face* magazine calls "[butt]-forward." But she's also not dressing for any man. She shoots the arrow. The entire set in front of her is lit up with flames. As she begins the song, the crowd sings along with her. A soldier hands her a sword; she confidently throws it back to him a few beats later. Her voice soars—when she sings "I told you so," it's full of righteous anger, and even people who aren't queer like her can feel the frustration of her unrequited love.

The 2024 festival season was an epic one for Chappell, beginning with her performance at Coachella on April 12.

"'Good Luck, Babe!' does not warrant me coming out with a weapon on fire," she admitted later to *The Guardian*. "But I was like, I have to do it. This is what I really would have wanted as my eleven-year-old boy version of myself." She laughed, and for a moment, the stress of being a megastar seemed to wash away. The audacious performance, which took place at the 2024 MTV Video Music Awards, was her first "big awards show." Not just performing at one, but attending a show that big. It was the year Chappell Roan blew up.

It was something she couldn't have ever foreseen for herself, not even when Atlantic Records signed her at seventeen, or when she moved to Los Angeles a few years later. "Don't turn into Miley," her friends and family warned her. Miley Cyrus had performed at the VMAs that year, in 2017, and everyone was recalling her scandalous 2013 performance, when she shed her Hannah Montana persona. "The foam finger rocked my world," Chappell told podcast host Adam Lisicky. But "for my conservative, very modest community, that was a huge no-no. Like, that is not OK, especially Miley coming from Hannah Montana to that, her authentic self. People were very concerned of me becoming that." And so that is exactly what she set out to become.

Chappell is best known for her upbeat pop anthems—but she began her career singing ballads, as seen here during her Midwest Princess Tour stop in Fort Lauderdale, Florida, October 26, 2023.

FOLLOWING
Chappell takes the stage at the 2024 MTV Video Music Awards, a knight in shining armor to fans across the world.

"'Good Luck, Babe!' does not warrant me coming out with a weapon on fire. But I was like, I have to do it. This is what I really would have wanted as my eleven-year-old boy version of myself."

TRACK 1

A GIRL NAMED KAYLEIGH

In Willard, Missouri, a farming community of just over five thousand people, Chappell once described it by saying, "There's more cows than people." Springfield, Missouri, the closest city, was just like the other Springfields all over the Midwest: it had a decent hospital, some well-regarded Christian colleges, and clean parks interspersed with America's most popular chain stores. It was even home to the original Bass Pro Shop and a wildlife museum-aquarium that shared its parking lot. It was cold in the winter; hot in the summer. Nice, some might say. Willard was also full of good people—most of them, the same.

On February 19, 1998, Kayleigh Rose Amstutz was born. Her parents, Springfield locals Dwight and Kara Amstutz, were still in college. Dwight, a navy veteran, became a registered nurse. Kara—who has the same curly hair and light, blue-gray eyes as her daughter—would become a veterinarian. They had three kids after Kayleigh, and settled in Willard, near their own parents. It was what you might call a "normal," or "middle American" family.

Kayleigh loved the peacefulness of Willard—beautiful, open, and easy to access nature where she grew up learning to catch frogs in the creek. With a quiet childhood, Springfield—nestled in the heart of the Ozark Mountains—didn't seem so bad either. But "I never quite felt like it was where I [was] meant to be. I didn't connect with a lot of people my age there," Chappell later told podcast host Adam Lisicky. "I feel like I didn't fit in well there because I was super creative and the biggest thing that happened there every week was like Friday night football [or] high school football." She also felt depressed and angry, even as a child. Her grades were OK, but she frequently acted out. Kayleigh got in trouble, fought

PREVIOUS
Chappell rocks one of her trademarks, a cowboy hat, at the House of Blues in Chicago, October 2023.

> "I feel like I didn't fit in well there because I was super creative and the biggest thing that happened there every week was like Friday night football."

with her parents, and even kicked a hole in the wall. Back then, she and her parents had no idea why she was having extreme mood swings, why she felt the need to act aggressively, or simply wasn't happy. "I think my parents just thought I was being a brat, so I had such a difficult time," she said. They tried bringing her to therapy, but it was a stop-and-start process. "All my parents could do was try their best." Later, she would be diagnosed with bipolar disorder.

After many years, once Chappell had become a pop star, *The Face* magazine would ask her if she was "the type of kid who put on cartwheel-inflected dances to Britney Spears in the family basement." *The Face* wrote of Chappell's reaction: "Her whole face softens at the assumption."

"I wish I was that girl," Chappell said. Later, she told *The Guardian*, "I was very mentally ill–suicidal for years–and not medicated, because that's just not a part of Midwest culture. It's not: Maybe we should get you a psychiatrist. It's: You need God. You need to pray about that."

She went to church three times a week, but the teachings there didn't provide any clarity. Later, she would tell *Rolling Stone*, "I felt so out of place in my hometown . . . I wish it was better. I wish I had better things to say. But mentally, I had a really tough time."

A writer would ask her if she was "the type of kid who put on cartwheel-inflected dances to Britney Spears in the family basement."

"I wish I was that girl," Chappell said.

The Kayleigh No One Knew

As she grew into her teenage years, things didn't get any better. She rebelled in small ways–snuck out of the house, tried smoking cigarettes, and, most importantly, secretly downloaded the Pandora app. She would put on her headphones and listen to music for hours–not Christian rock but Lana Del Rey, Lady Gaga, Lorde, and Ellie Goulding. She even got into hip-hop. "I would sit in my bathroom and just listen to Drake," she told *Variety*. "It was just a brand new world that I had not been exposed to ever. Hip-hop made me feel really cool and was a place where I could put all these angsty feelings. It still makes me feel that way."

Kayleigh had a lot of angsty feelings to struggle through–"being good," her anger deep inside, and just feeling like a bad person. "I just wanted to feel like a good person, but I had this part of me that wanted to escape so bad. I just wanted to scream . . . it was just this dichotomy of trying to be a good girl, but also wanting to freaking light things on fire."

It was when she was in seventh grade, when she felt like boys never had crushes on her, that she wondered why. And a thought crossed her mind: "Maybe I like girls." But she also felt that "I was only meant to be a mother or a wife and a loyal woman of God, and if I wasn't those things then I was nothing," she later told queer site *Qburgh*. She didn't know many women who hadn't followed that path, and she *especially* didn't know any women who dated other women. "There was no queer representation," Chappell said of Willard. "I didn't know a single out lesbian girl, gay girl, bi girl, nothing." She knew that she thought girls were prettier, nicer, and more fun to hang out with. But was it anything more?

If it was, it wasn't something she wanted to probe. "There were a couple of gay boys in my school who were out, and they got terrorized, slurred, threatened. I mean, it was horrible. I saw what would happen if you came out, and I knew that it was a sin at the time," she said. So, it became just another secret part of herself—one that felt more like a guilty pleasure, maybe even a joke. She later told *Teen Vogue*, "That was in the back of my head for all of high school: 'I think I like girls.' I didn't know how to deal with that part of myself except to make fun of it. 'Haha. It's so funny. It's a phase. Haha.'"

"That was in the back of my head for all of high school. 'I think I like girls.' I didn't know how to deal with that part of myself except to make fun of it."

Reflecting on it later, she felt like her narrow-minded community was much to blame. "There were so many things that I had to get over that I just deemed impossible for myself, and I think a lot of it came from my community that I grew up in, just not really supporting women in the way that helped women grow out of what served men," she told *Qburgh*. Women in Christian communities like Willard were often told that their greatest value came from their service to their family. It would have seemed ridiculous to think that instead Kayleigh Rose Amstutz was destined to inspire women—millions of women—to break free of the male gaze and just sing (or scream), to dress "silly" with no fear, to dance with joy . . . and to date their best-girl-friend instead of that guy they just met at the club. It would have seemed especially ridiculous to Kayleigh herself.

"I look back at myself and think about this girl who was really self-conscious, not confident," Chappell would say in a documentary made years later while looking through photos at her childhood home. Coming to a photo of her preteen self in cowboy boots, she remembers that a girl made fun of her for wearing them, so she stopped. "I still feel really self-conscious on stage sometimes, but I'm doing it for the version of me in the cowboy boots," she said.

FOLLOWING
Chappell attends Universal Music Group's 2023 Grammy after-party at Milk Studios Los Angeles on February 5, 2023.

"I just wanted to feel like a good person, but I had this part of me that wanted to escape so bad. I just wanted to scream... it was just this dichotomy of trying to be a good girl, but also wanting to freaking light things on fire."

A Voice Like "Whoa"

Everything changed for Chappell when she attended a summer camp in Michigan devoted to the arts, called Interlochen.

By then, she knew she had a natural talent for singing. She had started taking piano lessons around the age of eleven, and when she performed at her middle school talent show at thirteen, she decided to sing along with the song she played. Since it was the holiday season, she chose "The Christmas Song," and sang it with such feeling that every one of her grandparents in attendance cried. She had never performed in public, and no one (not even her) had realized that she naturally had an incredible singing voice. Chappell recalled later to *V* magazine, "I really wasn't in choir. I was in one year of choir my whole career of school, and some musical theater, but I [had] just started." Yet, she won the show.

The unexpected win encouraged her to enter more talent shows, big and small. She and her mother traveled to Austin for an *America's Got Talent* casting call, but she didn't make it past the first round. And when she tried out for *The Voice*, the producer she auditioned for didn't even look up at her. But at a local talent competition held at a Springfield hotel, she won $1,000 for her cover of Cyndi Lauper's "True Colors."

Her mom got her gigs at church services, country clubs, and the Willard Freedom Fest. Sometimes, they'd pay her piano teacher to accompany her. She did covers, mostly folk-rock from the '70s. "It was crazy . . ." she would later tell Adam Lisicky. "I was fourteen and I did, like, Carol Kane. People my age would be like, 'Who? I've never heard this in my life.'" Then, falling in love with the movement, emotion, and piano in "Stay" by Rihanna, she was inspired to start writing her own songs. But none of it seemed to click until she went to Interlochen.

She'd been to church camp before (many times), but this was something completely new. Attending Interlochen the summer between her sophomore and junior years of high school, Kayleigh suddenly realized there were people in the world who thought, felt, and acted just like her—they were artists. "It was the first time I'd ever been around creative kids," she would later tell *Vanity Fair*. Chappell was the only person in her extended family who played music, and she just didn't seem to fit in with the artsy kids at school. Even the teacher in charge of the Thespians Club didn't seem to like her. She ran cross country, but that's probably the most solitary team sport you can find. In a word, she was introverted.

At arts camp, so many kids were creative like her, and she felt like she belonged. For the first time, she was truly free to explore her creativity, wherever it would take her. Ten years later, *Rolling Stone* would write, "Chappell Roan was born, you might say, at a summer camp in 2014." There, she learned the art of songwriting, but her natural talent was already taking her far. "She arrived with Lennon–McCartney-level songwriting skills," the camp's director told the magazine.

> *"She arrived with Lennon-McCartney-level songwriting skills,"* the camp's director told **Rolling Stone**.

On July 17, she took part in a singer-songwriter showcase at Interlochen, singing her new original piece "Die Young." In the future, most people would consider it the first Chappell Roan song ever. It seemed wholly beyond her sixteen years. "My voice at the time was very strange to come out of my body, because I was very small, and very young, and it's quite deep and very different from my talking voice," she later explained to Lisicky. But it was more than that. What came out of her body wasn't just a grown-up voice, but a grown-up lament about the hopelessness of trying to help a reckless teenager—even though she had only set out to write a song about her friends smoking cigarettes.

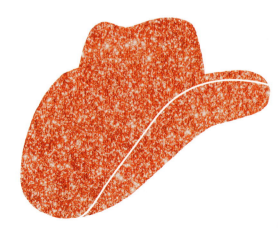

The Whirlwind and the Deal

Before Chappell was a singer, she was a performer. Enrolled in a local acting class in Springfield, her teacher noticed her stage presence even as a preteen and put her in touch with some acting managers in Los Angeles. They signed her, but it didn't mean much—Chappell and her family didn't want to move to LA, and there wasn't any professional acting to do in Springfield. So, they suggested that, for the time being, she should focus on music instead. She could upload her songs to social media and start to build a following there.

Chappell uploaded "Die Young" to YouTube under the name Kayleigh Rose, and her managers began sending it around. Her instructors at Interlochen weren't the only ones who were impressed. Troye Sivan, a popular Australian artist, reposted the video saying he had it "on repeat" for months. "I haven't heard a voice like this since Adele, no exaggeration," he wrote in all caps. Less than six months later, she was getting calls from record labels.

It all happened so fast—Republic Records asked her if she wanted to audition for them, and then flew her out to New York. While she was there, her family got calls from Columbia, Capitol, and Atlantic Records. They'd heard of her, and wanted to hear her perform in person. Her voice was called "smoky" and "sensual," and they compared her to Sia, Lorde, and Lana Del Rey. She was on her way to becoming a product, but in

"I was just sharing. I didn't know that I was gonna get discovered months after that."

her head, she had just written a song at camp and posted it on YouTube. "I was just sharing. I didn't know that I was gonna get discovered months after that," she told *Vanity Fair*. "It was very dramatic."

Chappell's managers didn't know anything about navigating the music business, and her family didn't have anyone they could ask for advice. It was a "whirlwind," she remembered, a fracturing of normal into new. She saw skyscrapers and the ocean for the first time, sang songs for some of the most impressive bigwigs in the music business, and struggled to finish her homework on time.

Eventually, she signed with Atlantic for a five-year deal. She simply liked what they had to say, especially the A&R (artists and repertoire) team, which focused on developing artists. A legendary label that had worked with everyone from Aretha Franklin to Bruno Mars, Atlantic must have seemed like a colossal opportunity at the time. But years later, Chappell would call it a "horrible, horrible deal" and "very predatory" on the podcast *Q with Tom Power*. Chappell had managed to find some kind of lightning in a bottle that the executives were looking for, but no matter how talented she was, she found that the balance of power was intrinsically in their favor. Not only did they control the development and production of her art, but they knew the business inside and out. They knew (or could have predicted) what the rest of her teenage years were going to look like; she didn't. "It's bizarre and should be illegal," she told Power. "I didn't know any better. I was a little kid. I was literally a minor."

PREVIOUS
Chappell shows off her creativity during an appearance on *The Late Show With Stephen Colbert* in 2024.

> *"I just didn't know how to process it, and sometimes I still don't know how to process it."*

"I just didn't know how to process it, and sometimes I still don't know how to process it," she confessed to *Headliner* in her twenties. Her school trumpeted it in the same sentence as the lunch menu over the PA system with the morning announcements. "I just had my head in my hands," she told Lisicky, "and a lot of people thought it was fake." With a bigtime contract, high school didn't seem feasible (or necessary) anymore, and her parents arranged for her to get her final credits online. When she had passed all her classes, her record-signing party doubled as her graduation party.

Once she could, Atlantic sent her to write with top producers, flying her to New York and Los Angeles with one of her parents every six weeks. It was overwhelming and a completely new learning curve she was just thrust into. She didn't know the structure of a pop song, or how to successfully collaborate, and she simply didn't know how to connect. In Chappellese, "I was just so [freaking] young, and it just sucked. But I did learn so much" she would later tell *Vanity Fair*.

Much of what she learned, she taught herself. Atlantic didn't provide her with vocal lessons, so she played songs by her favorite older singers, Karen Carpenter and Stevie Nicks, and tried to sing like them. Then she tried to combine the two. She even got into yodeling and incorporated that into her sound. "At the very beginning, I was doing a lot of dark-synth pop. It was ballady, witchy, and melodramatic," she told *Pop Crave*. After she became famous, *Vulture* would call it "moody, stripped down, singer-songwriter fare." *Pitchfork* would say "on early songs she sounds like she's nursing a shot of whiskey in a church basement."

Never a fan of school, she didn't miss it too much, but "I mourn being a kid," she lamented to *Vanity Fair*. "My career took that away from me pretty immediately when I signed." The teenagers in Willard felt even further away from her than her professional peers. She didn't feel comfortable talking about her struggles as a recording artist, and rumors that she was lying about her Atlantic contract persisted. She began to feel like she had done something taboo, and she worried that even when she *was* ready to release her new music, she was leaving herself exposed to the entire world, with all of her thoughts and feelings laid bare for the world to see.

It would be terrifying for anyone, but for a teenager who was still struggling with an undiagnosed bipolar disorder, Chappell felt intense pressure. "When you're bipolar and severely depressed, there [are] so many lies that depression tells you," she told Power. At that age, she didn't know how to say "no" or how to protect her mental health, and the change in her lifestyle felt more than abrupt. She would later describe the feeling to *Variety* as "very unhinged and really scary."

"I mourn being a kid. My career took that away from me pretty immediately when I signed."

Overwhelmed in Los Angeles but anxious from all the attention in her hometown, Chappell felt most at home, perhaps, when working on her music. To her, it was making art, and she'd hole herself up in her room until her sister would knock on her door to tell her dinner was ready. "It may take three hours to write a song, and other times three months," she told music site *AXS* at the time. "It all depends on the feeling." She wrote songs that were extremely personal to her—usually about her teenage boyfriends—and just hoped that people would connect with them. "I was so desperate to feel understood," she later said about the period to *The Guardian*.

In addition to working on individual songs, Kayleigh also worked in the studio to perfect her overall sound. Who did she want to be as an artist? While some family members encouraged her to go with a Christian-rock or country sound, ultimately, she went with a "very moody vibe" that she described to *AXS* as "dark pop with some influences of the sixties and seventies." She also decided she needed a stage name.

FOLLOWING
When Chappell began her career, she was still a long way from what would become her iconic look: clown-white face, blazing red hair, and unique costumes like this one from 2024's Boston Calling Music Festival.

"It may take three hours to write a song, and other times three months. It all depends on the feeling."

The Birth of Chappell Roan

While Kayleigh was working on perfecting her sound, her family was facing a tragedy: Her mom's father, Dennis Chappell, was losing his battle with brain cancer. "He's just so proud of our family, and he was really supportive of me," she told the *Springfield News-Leader*. Later, she'd say on her YouTube channel, "People would always ask if I had a plan B and he never asked. [He] just knew I could do it and so I decided to make myself Chappell after him." She played him some of her rough demos, and told him that for her stage name, she wanted to use his last name in his honor.

On August 7, 2017, "Good Hurt," the first song by Chappell Roan was released. Reviewed in a handful of publications, *Interview* magazine said it was "a strong indicator of her imminent popularity" and UK site One Stop Record Shop called it "indulgent and menacing, powerful enough to leave you branded a Roan addict."

The following month, School Nights, Chappell's first EP, was released. On September 28, she set out on her first tour, as an opening act for Australian singer Vance Joy. Traveling the US and Canada in a rented van (which she was too young to drive), she and her guitar player traveled to fourteen major cities. Then, in early 2018, she toured with Declan McKenna, a British artist known for his energetic shows. Hitting smaller cities like Hamden, Connecticut; Akron, Ohio; and Decatur, Georgia, they played forty-six shows in two months.

What's a Roan?

"Roan," the second half of Chappell's stage name, is one of those strange words that's never used all by itself. But "strawberry roan" or "chestnut roan" is used to describe a horse that has a coloring that mixes white and reddish-brown. They're not quite "pink ponies," but they're just about as close as you can come to one in real life.

These beautiful and unique horses inspired "The Strawberry Roan," a ballad written in 1915 by Curley Fletcher and popularized during the Depression when the song became a book (and later, the title of several movies). The original song is about a rodeo rider who tries to break a horse that refuses to be broken. It is a strawberry roan that he wholeheartedly claims is "a regular outlaw." Not only was it Chappell's grandfather's favorite song, but it's also a perfect last name for her persona.

In an interview after her first show opening for Declan in Texas, Chappell gushed to Austin Underground Inc., "That was the funnest show I've ever done. I'm not used to dancing around on stage because I think I'm a bad dancer, but I was like eh, I don't care, I'm just going to wiggle around. It was such a blast, and the crowd was fantastic."

But the songs on School Nights didn't lend themselves well to dancing. "I hated performing my old EP on tour," she later confessed to *Vulture*. Her "dark alt-pop girl vibe" was "really, just not fun" she told *Qburgh*. And whenever she watched Declan perform, she was jealous. "He would jump off the speakers, and throw balloons in the crowd, and have so much fun every night," she told *Vulture*. "I was like, I want to do that. I don't want to do what I'm doing. This is too serious. How do I have fun on stage?" She loved performing, but she wanted to perform in a different way. There was only one problem: She was almost finished with her first full-length album, and it was full of songs she didn't want to play.

Nineteen-year-old Chappell Roan opens for Vance Joy at the Seattle Showbox in 2017 during a fourteen-stop tour.

Chappell's Influences

Childhood Kitsch

No matter what pop culture inspires her in the current moment, Chappell keeps her childhood self as her guiding star. The question she asks herself most often about her work is: "Is this what would've made little me happy?"

Her fans would not be surprised to hear that, mainly, it consists of pink glitter. "I wanted everything to be pink, purple sparkle," she told *Vanity Fair* about her childhood. But then she started to reject traditional femininity: "Once I got into fifth grade, it was like basketball shorts." Her current aesthetic is often a combo of both of these worlds: riding a bedazzled dirt bike (in a matching outfit) for the "Femininomenon" cover, having "Midwest Princess" emblazoned on camo hats for her tour merch, or wearing a sexy luchador costume during her Lollapalooza performance.

Although today she describes her look as more Bratz Dolls, growing up she loved Barbies, including the animated Barbie movies from the 2000s, and *Spy Kids*.

In addition to bedazzling just about everything, she brings out elements of her childhood in other ways: fake stickers on a tour poster, a prom-themed cover album, jewelry from Claire's, and more. As for makeup, her features are exaggerated—which is a nod to drag, but also to clowns and the big ideas of a little mind. As she told *Rolling Stone* in her first cover interview, "If a five-year-old could draw a pop star, it would be me."

Chappell performs at Lollapalooza on August 1, 2024 in a kitschy, lucha libre costume.

TRACK 2

PART-TIME POP STAR

Today, the Abbey defines the gay enclave of West Hollywood. But once, it was just the dream of David Cooley, who opened a LGBTQ+-centric bakery alongside a dry cleaner's in 1991. At the height of the AIDS crisis, he created a safe space where the neighborhood could come together around the cramped wooden bar for community, activism, and an egg dish he made using a laundry steamer. Soon, he got a liquor license and moved the business across the street, upgrading to a space that had an outdoor patio. There, his customers could not only enjoy the beautiful weather but also be seen by the community. "This is the first time people were actually exposed to the outside, where people driving by could see them, where no one was starting to be afraid. It's okay to be who you are. That was a big step," David remembered while speaking to KCRW Los Angeles.

By the time Chappell stepped foot into the Abbey Food and Bar in the summer of 2018, it was truly an impressive space. It had expanded to 16,000 square feet (1,486 square meters) and included a huge bar area, two dance floors, cabanas out back, and a café that hearkened back to its original roots. Since it was added onto little by little, different parts of the Abbey feel different, and if you stay there all day, you're likely to be greeted by all sorts of different vibes (and it's LA, so there are always vibes), from a lighthearted brunch full of drag performers to evening DJs. Celebrity sightings are common—even people who find the Abbey overly glam or vapid eventually find themselves there. It's an institution, after all.

PREVIOUS
Chappell performs at Outside Lands at Golden Gate Park on August 11, 2024.

The first night that Chappell stepped foot through the door, shortly after her twenty-first birthday, she had been living in Los Angeles for about six months. She had packed everything into her car and drove three days straight to move in with some friends from Interlochen who were pursuing jobs in film. Now she was trying to make it work among the thousands of young artists who move to LA every year.

It had been hard for her family to see her go, especially her mom, but it was even harder for Chappell herself. She missed the seasons, and how simple everything seemed back home. She had a hard time finding a friend group, parties gave her anxiety, and she didn't feel like she fit into the pop-writing industry. "It's just very lonely to move to a new city when you're in such a difficult industry and so young," she later told *Capital Buzz*.

Making use of her age privileges, she went out to bars and clubs, and she soon found that going out late and socializing with others who wanted to enjoy life could be pretty fun. "I was told this city is demonic and Satanists live here," she later told *NME*. "But when I got to West Hollywood, it opened my eyes [to the fact] that everything I was afraid of wasn't always true—especially about the queer community."

"When I got to West Hollywood, it opened my eyes [to the fact] that everything I was afraid of wasn't always true—especially about the queer community."

When Chappell walked into the Abbey for the first time, she was in awe. "It was like what I thought the holy spirit was supposed to feel like," she told Adam Lisicky. "I was absolutely enthralled. It was everything I was taught it wasn't. It was magic. And I just couldn't get over it." The bar was packed, full of people she had never seen in Missouri: men dressed in fabulously feminine outfits, friends outdoing each other with how flamboyantly they could tell a story, people of the same sex kissing and holding hands. Most of all, she saw people just enjoying being themselves.

And no one seemed to enjoy being themselves more than the go-go dancers performing on platforms around the room. They were everything Chappell was told was bad—and yet they were bringing joy to everyone around them. They were confident and free, and she wondered if she had it inside herself to be able to do something like that. "I was sober the entire night!" she later told *Headliner* of her spiritual awakening. "I needed to experience it sober. I danced my [butt] off and I didn't care; it was one of the most fun nights ever . . . I just felt like I belonged there, and that really changed my life."

"I danced my [butt] off and I didn't care, it was one of the most fun nights ever... I just felt like I belonged there, and that really changed my life."

Enter Dan Nigro

That year, 2018, had been a hard one for Chappell. Not only was she trying to start over somewhere new, but the album she had finished (the one she was so unenthusiastic about) was scrapped by Atlantic. "They shelved [it] and told me I needed to start over," she said on Adam Lisicky's podcast. She expounded, "The system isn't set up to grow baby artists. It's made to grow artists that are doing well and make them do better." But she was actually glad and felt like it was for the best. She still didn't like the songs she was putting out, including her recent single "Bitter." And she knew something had to change.

"I just felt like I was failing over and over and over again because we could never get a song, or a song wasn't good," she told Adam. Even though they were pairing her with great producers (like Joel Little, who produced Lorde), "I didn't know what I wanted, because I didn't know I was supposed to know what I wanted," she explained. "I just thought we were going to talk, and write a song; I didn't know how to get there though."

Chappell and her producer/cowriter, Dan Nigro, attend a panel discussion at the Grammy Museum on November 7, 2024.

> *"I didn't know what I wanted, because I didn't know I was supposed to know what I wanted."*

That all changed when she met songwriter and producer Dan Nigro. Originally from Long Island, New York, Dan had started off in the music industry when he was nineteen, getting signed to Triple Crown Records with his emo band As Tall as Lions. After they broke up for creative reasons, he gave songwriting and producing a shot. He had success cowriting Sky Ferreira's "You're Not the One" and Kylie Minogue's "If Only," and found that he enjoyed the process of helping artists (who were completely unlike him) find their unique sound.

When Dan and Chappell were brought together by their managers in October 2018, they didn't know what to expect. That very first session, they wrote a song called "Love Me Anyway," about loving someone despite their faults. Dan was so impressed that they booked two more days together in the studio. Later, Chappell would reflect to *Vulture*, "It's interesting because Dan is a forty-year-old straight white man. I don't know how it works, but I feel like I bring the queer perspective, the pop, and he brings the technical perspective and pushes me lyrically." Of Chappell, Dan would later say to *Hits Daily Double*, "She's a great lyricist. She writes amazing concepts. I'm really good with melodies and chords, and we really complement each other."

The second day was even more prolific than the first. Together, they wrote "California," a sad song that expressed Chappell's disillusionment with her new life and her longing to be back home. "It felt magical and deeply relatable," he later told *Billboard*. He felt the song was important, and he knew it felt that way because of Chappell. "I had this feeling like I was a part of something deeply special," he said. The writing sessions became some of his favorites of his career.

Dan was so excited about "Love Me Anyway" and "California" that he wanted to show them off to Chappell's team at Atlantic Records. "So I invited them over," he later recalled to *Hits Daily Double*. "I printed out the lyrics to 'California,' which is all a cappella for the first twenty seconds. I wanted them to sit in the room and listen to the song and look at the lyrics." Dan was sure they'd be as awed as he was. "But one of the A&R people didn't show up to the meeting. That was the first of many disappointments [when] trying to get them to be involved in the project. Then they canceled another meeting."

But it didn't matter. Who cared if the executives didn't see the brilliance of "Love Me Anyway," or barely even wanted to hear "California"? Dan was inspired by their collaboration and knew they could do more. "I was convinced she was my favorite songwriter that I had ever worked with," Dan recalled, and so they kept writing together.

All the while, Chappell was still on a mission to discover her true sound—who she really wanted to be as an artist. She thought back to Declan McKenna's exuberance on stage, and the freedom of the go-go dancers at the Abbey, and the pop singers she loved, growing up, like Lady Gaga,

Kesha, and Katy Perry. She wanted something people could party to—preferably something she could perform while wearing weird outfits.

Instead, she found writing pop songs even harder than writing ballads. "It takes a lot of creative talent to make a song mean something but also feel like bubbles," she explained to Sam Prance at *Capital Buzz*. The things she wrote felt funny, not important, and there was a certain campiness about pop songs that she found hard to wrap her head around at first. "Until I moved to LA and West Hollywood, I wasn't really aware of how campy life could be," she recalled. Back home in Willard, everyone was so reserved. But when she went to places like the Abbey, she realized, "Why am I so serious? Everyone is having so much fun."

Even though she was homesick, LA proved to be the perfect place to explore herself as a person. "All of a sudden I realized I could truly be any way I wanted to be, and no one would bat an eye," she told *Headliner*. A thousand miles away from Willard, she didn't have to take into account what her mother would think or worry that she was too much for people to handle. In Los Angeles, you had to be *extremely* weird to even be considered slightly weird. And she loved that.

With access to more vintage and thrift stores in LA than the entire state of Missouri, Chappell began experimenting more with her clothes. She went to drag shows, which she would later tell *Qburgh* was akin to "when I went to Disney World® when I was seven and I saw Princess Jasmine."

"Why am I so serious? Everyone is having so much fun."

As she was going about the city and discovering the possibilities of her new life, she was constantly asking herself what she truly valued. At the same time, she worked to perfect her sound.

"I wanted to be bold and say things that might be a little edgy," she recalled to Sam Prance. "I come from a super-conservative area where I wouldn't even wear the things that I wear in LA here in public—I would just feel weird about it. So I'm just going to be everything that I am in LA, in my music."

But it still didn't feel right. Shouldn't she be in her room, pouring her soul out until she had nothing left? Was it OK to simply have fun? Finally, she had a breakthrough. "What really made me feel like I could make silly art was once I got into therapy with inner child work, and [started] working on what did little me want? And that was a little girl who wanted to wear makeup, and dance, and be obnoxious," Later, she would tell *Vanity Fair*, "I had to let go of the adult in me that thought, 'Oh, I need to be so sophisticated and serious and so good at everything or else I'm not good enough.'" Once she did, "Pink Pony Club" was born.

FOLLOWING
Chappell's signature look soon came to include cherry-red hair, seen here while performing at Spotlight: A Night with Chappell Roan and Dan Nigro moderated by Brandi Carlile at Grammy Museum LA in 2024.

"I had to let go of the adult in me that thought, 'Oh, I need to be so sophisticated and serious and so good at everything or else I'm not good enough.'"

Pink Pony Pivot

The playful glissando at the beginning of "Pink Pony Club" warned listeners that this was not the typical Chappell Roan song. For the first several verses, she's still singing in her normal moody, understated way. Meanwhile, the piano continues to build. And there's something else—did she just say that boys can be queens? Suddenly, the chorus breaks. It's "Pink Pony Club"—a dance song, a gay anthem, a sing-along banger. It's the song that would change Chappell's entire career.

"It's like an American songbook standard," queer songwriter Justin Tranter would later tell *Hits Daily Double*. "This is possibly the best song ever written."

Composed on Valentine's Day 2019, it was the third song she and Dan wrote together. Inspired by the Abbey and a strip club from her hometown that had painted the outside of its building hot pink, it tells the story of a girl who finds joy dancing at the club even if her mother doesn't approve. Not only was it Chappell's first pop song, it was also the first song that wasn't ostensibly about Chappell herself—the character in the song mentions being from Tennessee and having a Southern drawl.

Endless Comparisons

Chappell is one of a kind, and that means she's been compared to just about everybody. Here's some of the varied artists she's been likened to.

Lorde. One of Chappell's favorite singers when she was young, it's no surprise that Lorde was a common comparison during Chappell's early career.

Robyn. *Paper* magazine likened Chappell's music to "early Robyn," while *Vulture* said the "Pink Pony Club" video "calls to mind a *Toddlers & Tiaras* interpretation of Robyn's 'Call Your Girlfriend' choreo."

Rina Sawayama. *American Songwriter* compared Chappell to this Japanese-British artist because of their singing voices and campy aesthetic.

Fiona Apple. *Paper* magazine asserted that it's Fiona Apple that Chappell most resembles, "with her penchant for creativity over accolades or the machinations of the Hollywood machine."

Taylor Swift. Fans on social media have long debated whether or not Chappell's voice sounds like Taylor's—and whose is better.

Cyndi Lauper. *Billboard* compared "Good Luck, Babe!" to a Cyndi Lauper song because of Chappell's big voice, big hair, and big choruses.

Elton John. British newspaper the *Independent* called Chappell "a star cut from Elton's cloth."

Chappell was having a blast working with Dan, and Dan felt he was working with someone whose music could make a difference in people's lives. "When we made 'Pink Pony Club,' that was the record where it felt like we were making something actively powerful," he later told *Billboard*. "It was that sort of feeling, where you get the sense that you're making a song that people need." Their managers loved it too. Chappell's manager Nick Bobetsky later recalled to *Hits Daily Double*, "When we all heard it, we looked at each other and were like, 'This is unbelievable.'" But Atlantic was still unenthused. They didn't like the concept of a young woman leaving home to self-righteously become a stripper. Dan was incredulous that they weren't behind the song wholeheartedly. "I remember thinking, 'Am I taking crazy pills?'"

Trusting in her collaborators, Chappell went forward with "Pink Pony Club" anyway. Even though she loved the song, it was still way out of her comfort zone. She told *Headliner*, "Even recording the vocals for that—I couldn't have anyone looking at me because I felt so out of place. But I knew I needed to do it. It was just uncomfortable, but I'm so glad that I pushed myself because this is exactly where I want to be."

"I knew I needed to do it. It was just uncomfortable, but I'm so glad that I pushed myself because this is exactly where I want to be."

The video was even more of a pivot from the look of other music videos she'd done, which Chappell once described to Adam Lisicky as "just me in a field, looking off very dramatically." Wearing a glittery white hat, leotard, and cowboy boots under a tasseled leather jacket, in the "Pink Pony Club" music video Chappell shimmies her way around a half-empty biker bar as the song amps up. "We shot it pretty much in order," she told *Headliner*. "That nervousness that you see is 100 percent real—I was absolutely terrified. I'm not a dancer—I've never been strong at it, and I just knew I had to just not care . . . but it was hard to not care."

Fortunately, the nervousness works for the character, who does an awkward thrust over the mic stand and some strange moves while slithering around on the floor. But soon, the video shifts to what she sees in her own mind, which is a disco ball, go-go dancers, and the drag queen Porkchop Parker playing the guitar. Once the jacket comes off, literally, Chappell finds her groove, with the dancers lifting her in the air and spinning her around. "I've always wanted to do that. It was like my dream to lose it and dance my ass off," she enthused.

Chappell had completely left her comfort zone, and the result was art that made her feel free. Dan knew it would have the same effect on listeners, but Atlantic couldn't be convinced. They were afraid it would alienate her audience, and they advised her not to release it. Because of their worry, all of a sudden, the risk started to feel like a mistake to Chappell herself. She later told *Variety*, "I was embarrassed by it because I was like, 'This is so cheesy!' And at that point, I was confusing cheesy and campy."

> *"I was scared because I felt like it wasn't going to be accepted for some reason, or that people would hate me."*

Chappell felt like she had finally found the fun sound she was looking for, but she wasn't confident she had pulled it off. "I just was going back and forth," she later told *Headliner*. "I was embarrassed! My team is so good, and they worked really hard on it, and I worked hard on it. I was scared because I felt like it wasn't going to be accepted for some reason, or that people would hate me." But she decided to trust her gut, and in April 2020, the single was finally released. But the timing couldn't have been worse.

The world had just been shut down due to the COVID-19 pandemic, and there were no clubs open to play her club song. The fans seemed to love it, but Atlantic was still not happy. They were equally unimpressed with the numbers when they released "Love Me Anyway" and "California," Chappell's other two collaborations with Dan. On top of that, Chappell couldn't tour, which is often how artists make money for labels, and so, like many artists in 2020, she got dropped.

Chappell had mixed feelings. She had been unhappy during her time with the company, but in a way, after being removed from their list, she just felt worse. She went into detail about the time on Adam's podcast: "Even though I didn't want to admit it, I wasn't happy, and I was very trapped, and I didn't feel heard. I think the people on my team did the best that they could, but unfortunately, in the label system, it's not your team that makes the decisions, it's the people who have the money at the top, and all they can look at is numbers. And so, when my team would turn in the reports, they would see that, 'Oh, Chappell is not making the money that we need her to make,' and so, in return, wouldn't give me the budgets I needed to push my career forward. So it was sad all around. I was sad before I got dropped; I was sad after I got dropped... I [felt] like a failure."

When she was at her lowest, somehow, a glimmer of hope: a diagnosis for bipolar II disorder. Suddenly, things started making sense on a personal level, even among the chaos of the global pandemic. The question now was what to do next.

"I really thought I would come to LA and all my dreams would come true, and I would feel so like myself, and at times it was that, but for many years it was so depressive, and so heartbreaking, and I felt so defeated," she later told Sam Prance. Ultimately, she was left with a feeling of "wanting my dad to come pick me up, and just like, 'get me out of California,' because I felt like I let myself down." And so, she went home to Willard.

FOLLOWING
Chappell performs at the Grammy Museum in Los Angeles, California, on November 7, 2024.

"When we made 'Pink Pony Club,' that was the record where it felt like we were making something actively powerful," Dan told **Billboard**.

COVID at the Coffee Kiosk

To anyone who's seen Chappell Roan perform "Pink Pony Club" to a crowd of thousands, the thought that she would be working at a coffee shop shortly after releasing the song seems unfathomable. But that's exactly what she did. And it wasn't even a *shop*, it was a *kiosk*, situated in an isolated part of the parking lot where customers could easily drive through. A popular chain in Springfield that specialized in candy bar–style frappés, they had what Chappell called "the worst coffee in the world." Management required that every drink be completed in fewer than sixty seconds.

While the world was locked down, Chappell entertained herself by learning new crafts and doing Instagram Lives. She held "live slumber parties" for her fans and let audience members share the screen to tell stories about first kisses and awkward dates. She kept writing things down in her Notes app, knowing it would be inspiration for further songs. And like many people in 2020, she started dating someone long-distance over the internet.

Continuing to struggle with her mental health, she had started attending therapy, sometimes even bringing her parents to sessions. "It saved us," she later told *Rolling Stone*. "I was like, 'I can't go my whole life hating my parents for not knowing how to handle a really, really sick child.'"

She found forgiveness, and they found understanding. And while that was all happening, Chappell kept writing.

She mulled over her options: She thought about going to college, maybe moving to New York or Nashville. She even contemplated leaving the music industry. She always thought she'd make a good esthetician; maybe an art therapist. There was nothing guiding her, and it was safe to say that she had no idea what came next. "I was just kind of like, 'I wonder if this is really for me,'" she later told *Q with Tom Power*. "I knew I liked how 'Pink Pony Club' made me feel, but I didn't know how to access that feeling again, because I wrote it when I was at a club, when I was around people, when I was having a great time." In her mind, she knew that if she wanted to finish the songs she had started fiddling with in her head and on her phone, she needed to go back to LA. She decided to give herself one more chance.

"It felt like I needed to get out of Missouri to finish the rest of the songs that needed to be written," she told *Vanity Fair*. "I couldn't write pop songs when I was depressed on a farm."

In October 2020, Chappell gave herself one year to see how far she could get as an artist. Just one year to decide if that was the life for her or not. So, she packed her car and headed back to California for the second time.

FOLLOWING
Chappell performs "Pink Pony Club" onstage at the 67th Annual Grammy Awards on February 2, 2025.

"It felt like I needed to get out of Missouri to finish the rest of the songs that needed to be written."

The Pop Star at the Donut Shop

By November 2021, Chappell felt like she had gotten practically nowhere. After she moved back to LA, she worked as a nanny, was a production assistant on a TV show, and taught songwriting to teenagers for a summer at Interlochen. Now, she was working at a vegan café called Donut Friend, where the donuts all had indie rock–themed names like "Green Teagan and Sara" and "Jimmy Eat Swirl." The year limit she had given herself had already come and gone, but she told herself to keep going, even though it wasn't easy—on top of her challenges with the music industry, she was still struggling to find the best medications to treat her bipolar disorder. During her first year back, she spent a lot of time in bed, crying.

Meanwhile, since she and Dan had written "Pink Pony Club," he'd not only gotten married to the love of his life, he'd also become one of the hottest writer-producers in town, thanks to the massive success of his collaboration with breakout artist Olivia Rodrigo. Dan stumbled upon Olivia online, loved her voice, and contacted her on Instagram to see if she was interested in collaborating. He turned out to be as great a partner for her as he was for Chappell. "He gets me and realizes where I want to take the music sonically," Olivia recalled to *Fast Company*. "There was a familiarity and comfort there that in turn supported the creative process and my confidence as a songwriter."

The first collaboration that they released, "Drivers License," became a pandemic-era smash hit. (Chappell, who had heard "Drivers License" before it was released, had always known it would be a hit, but was as shocked as everybody else.) In May, Olivia released her entire album, *Sour*, on which Dan had cowritten eight of the eleven songs. It soon cracked a record for the most-streamed album *ever* by a woman in the history of Spotify.

Chappell knew that Dan had become one of the most sought-after producers in LA overnight, but she was eager to get to work with him again. Although it was no "Drivers License," "Pink Pony Club" had become a cult hit, especially in queer circles, and it was only gaining steam.

The drag queen Trixie Mattel later reminisced to Chappell: "I showed it to a cool Gen Z person I know . . . and you know what? She said to me, and I will never recover: 'Yeah, like every white millennial gay guy has been showing me her.' It was like a game of telephone, the way you broke. It was like, really cool, where people knew first, and then they told other really cool queer people, and then they told other girls, and then they told people who work radio. It was this beautiful pyramid of people discovering you."

It wasn't long before every gay man in the know was singing along to "Pink Pony Club" whenever it came on. Talking about the song's cult status, Chappell told *Rolling Stone*, "It didn't surprise me. I was told very young that good art rises. And it's rising because it's good. So when I saw it was [rising], I was like, 'finally!' I don't even care if that makes me look [brazen], because it's not, I just simply think it's good." But she still had no label, no direction, and no songwriting partner she liked as much as Dan.

> *"It didn't surprise me. I was told very young that good art rises. And it's rising because it's good."*

After a little more than a year since she had moved back to LA, she finally met up with Dan to reignite their music collaboration. The first thing Chappell told him was how frustrated she was. "I was upset about my project not moving. I felt stuck and like no one was paying attention to me," she told *Rolling Stone*. "[Dan] was just looking at me and goes, 'You are going to run your career into the [freaking] ground if you don't start doing [stuff] on your own.'" For a singer who was plucked off YouTube at sixteen by a giant record label, then told to perform like their top artists until she was dropped, that advice must have come as a shock–the biggest challenge she had ever received by somebody who understood her music so well.

Chappell speaks about her collaboration with her producer, cowriter, and friend Dan Nigro at the Grammy Museum in 2024.
FOLLOWING
Chappell performs at Waterfront Park in Louisville for the 2024 Kentucky Pride Festival on June 15.

"[Dan] was just looking at me and goes, 'You are going to run your career into the [freaking] ground if you don't start doing [stuff] on your own.'"

Conceptualizing Chappell Roan

Chappell hated to call it "branding," but that's exactly what it was. Before she started putting out music again, she needed to create a persona that she would enjoy playing and that her fans would love watching. She wanted to be bold and outrageous, "[the] opposite of what the community had encouraged women to be" in Missouri, she'd later tell Adam Lisicky; "purposely tacky and trashy." Kayleigh started to envision Chappell Roan as "this rebellious version of myself that I never got to be." They thought she was crazy? She'd show them what crazy really was.

To help bring her reimagined Chappell to life, she enlisted a new friend, artist Ramisha (Misha) Sattar. Chappell and Misha had met online, when Chappell had seen some of her artwork on Instagram and asked for her help on a performance piece.

Misha, coincidentally, was also from the Midwest (she grew up in Nebraska), but she was unlike anybody Chappell had known in Missouri. She also loved to make collages, craft, go to thrift shops, and be creative. Together, they talked about what Chappell Roan needed, made mood boards, and used Bedazzlers to fasten gems to random outfits. But most of all, they just made each other laugh. "Ramisha is so inspiring to me," Chappell later told CNN. "We inspire each other, but I feel like she has opened so many doors emotionally for me with art and letting go." Pretty soon, they were best friends.

While Chappell brought a clear vision to the project, Misha brought a camp aesthetic that CNN would call "over the top, Gen-Z Lisa Frank–esque." She loved vintage materials, Hollywood glam, and troll dolls. Aspiring to be unique and fresh, her aim was to make art that made her feel good. "She is just as much Chappell Roan as I am, honestly," Kayleigh told CNN. "She is Chappell Roan too."

Chappell would later describe her character to *Rolling Stone* with big hair, bold makeup, and outrageous costumes. The new Chappell Roan was explosive, feminist, rhinestone-forward, and–in a word–obnoxious. "There isn't really a place for showmanship in Missouri in the way that I would like," she told website *Cherwell* the following year. "[Chappell]'s consciously camp . . . I don't think I would have been as outgoing and obnoxious if I had been from the coasts." The music magazine *Pitchfork* would later call it "campy, fabulous, and uninhibited–like a nightclub-going younger sister of Miss Frizzle."

> "I dont think I would have been as outgoing and obnoxious if I had been from the coasts."

Chappell's Influences

Country

When Chappell first performed "The Giver" on *Saturday Night Live* in 2024, fans weren't only surprised that she was singing an unreleased song—she was singing country. "I'm from southwest Missouri, grew up on Christian and country [music], and then found 'Alejandro' by Lady Gaga," she told Today's Country Radio about her influences. Other country inspirations include Jason Aldean, Alan Jackson, and—naturally—gay icon Dolly Parton. Dolly is "an artist that has embraced all of everyone," Chappell told Apple Music about the legend. "And no matter how we try to put music in certain genres and, 'I'm a country artist; I'm a pop artist,' it's like people can be fans of all of it and can go to all the concerts."

Like Dolly, Chappell sees herself across genres. She has no plans to release a full country album anytime soon, but as she told Today's Country Radio, "I have country in my heart." The cowboy hat has been a trademark of hers since "Pink Pony Club," and it's a mainstay of fan costumes at concerts. In her costumes, Chappell also makes liberal use of one of Dolly's favorites: rhinestones. Diamonds and Rhinestones is the title of one of Dolly's albums, and they're also mentioned in "The Giver," which was officially released on March 13, 2025.

Chappell performs at TD Garden as Olivia Rodrigo's opener for her GUTS World Tour in Boston, Massachusetts on April 1, 2024.

Although Dan had encouraged her to find her own voice, he had also helped Chappell make some headway in the music industry. First, he introduced her to Olivia, who immediately fell in love with her music. Chappell sang background vocals on some of her songs, and they became fast friends. Olivia even visited Chappell at Donut Friend, where they hung out and ate some rock 'n' roll donuts.

Dan had also been talking with Jennifer Knoepfle, an executive at Sony Music. Jennifer agreed to a publishing partnership with Chappell and Dan (which is different than a record deal), so they'd have easier avenues for distributing their music.

And for the first time in Chappell's career, the songs seemed to be coming fast and furious. Chappell and Dan were creating like they had never before, meeting regularly and writing new songs in pieces. Chappell trusted him enough to open up about the experiences she wanted to write about. Coming a long way from her first writing session at sixteen, there was a newfound confidence in singing in ways she'd never tried before. "I remember her walking into the studio one day and just flat-out saying 'I don't give a [care] about what people say anymore. If I like it, then it's good,'" Olivia told *Rolling Stone*. "I could tell she actually meant it, too. That's her magic." The magic was clearly happening as they started to plan out an entire album.

Discovering Her Independence

In retrospect, being dropped by Atlantic was the best thing that ever happened to Chappell's career. Without a label, "no one was telling me what to do," she told Sam Prance. As an independent artist, she found new creative freedom, listening to her inner child as well as the artists who inspired her. Her friend, visual artist Ryan Clemens, came on board to help her with the music video for her next single, "Naked in Manhattan," and another friend, Jackie-with-an-exclamation-point, would direct some mini-documentaries for her YouTube channel. Wishing she knew more about Photoshop, social media, and other aspects of the business, Chappell realized that if the people at the music label had figured it out, she could figure it out too. So, she taught herself, and her online following continued to grow. "It was affirming, but it was just so empowering," she remembered. "And I felt like, '[Dang], I *am* meant to do this, because it's working, even without a label.'"

Dan also saw an opportunity in her lack of a label. He recalled to *Hits Daily Double*, "The first time we talked about it, I said, 'This is going to be the most exciting time ever. Because now we have no restrictions. We don't have to listen to anybody.'"

> *"The first time we talked about it, I said, 'This is going to be the most exciting time ever. Because now we have no restrictions. We don't have to listen to anybody.'"*

Together, they created music that was campy, fun, and carried an empowering message. "I always try to push myself and how I write pop music," Chappell told *Earmilk* at the time. "I want to see if I can get away with being as ridiculous as I possibly can." Oftentimes, they'd write things she thought were too silly, or stupid. But when she returned to it later on, she loved what they had made.

"You have to write mostly bad songs to write good ones . . . and that is heartbreaking, because you're just like, 'Oh my God, this is horrible,'" she joked to Sam Prance. The duo wrote and rewrote, listened and re-listened. Chappell especially liked listening to her demos in different places, learning that the songs felt different to her depending on where she was.

While Dan and Chappell were completing four more songs—"Naked in Manhattan," "Femininomenon," "My Kink is Karma," and "Casual"—Olivia was tearing up the stage on the extremely successful Sour Tour. For her last stop in the US, she asked Chappell if she would open for her. "I love u SO MUCH Olivia & I can't wait !!!!" Chappell wrote on Instagram. Later, she would tell *NME* that Olivia was "an angel."

Chappell knew that one of her strengths was performing, but this would be the largest audience—nine thousand people—that she had ever performed in front of by far. Since COVID-19 restrictions had been lifted, she had done a few live performances of "Pink Pony Club," but for her eight-song opening set for Olivia, she would sing it plus the four new songs, which hadn't even been released.

On May 27, 2022, Chappell performed to a sold-out crowd at the Billy Graham Civic Auditorium in San Francisco, bouncing back and forth on stage wearing a pink two-piece leotard festooned with tassels and glitter. "The energy was so electric because a lot of her fans are younger than my fans," Chappell told Triple J Radio. But she later confessed to Adam Lisicky that she experienced a strange letdown afterward. With such a huge accomplishment, she thought she'd have the feeling that she had arrived somewhere. "I thought I'd be like, 'Ah, I'm here. I've been working my whole life to do this.' [But] I remember sitting in my hotel room after the concert and being like, 'So that was that?'" When she got offstage and found herself right where she was before, the disappointment was palpable. "In my heart I thought it would make me feel a level up, that I would level up somehow. But no, I was where I was the night before."

FOLLOWING
Chappell onstage at the 2024 Austin City Limits Music Festival on October 13.

"I want to see if I can get away with being as ridiculous as I possibly can."

TRACK 3

THE INCLUSIVE QUEEN

It seemed Kayleigh had some catching up to do when it came to Chappell. In her newly released songs, Chappell sang about how attracted she was to women, and that she was thoroughly exploring her sexuality. Meanwhile, Kayleigh had never even kissed a girl. She was a little prude by LA standards, and even still wore the purity ring she was given as a teenager (it was opal, and she thought it was pretty). About her Chappell persona, she told the Associated Press, "The reality is that I'm not like that at all. I'm really uncomfortable by sex scenes in movies, or when people flirt with me . . . The songs kind of give me the opportunity to act like that, and say that, and dress like that . . . It's all a rebellion. That's what it is." But one thing Kayleigh *did* have in common with Chappell was that they were both queer.

When she got back to LA, Chappell joined a dating app and, at the suggestion of her therapist, went on a lot of dates to see if she could make a connection with someone. She went out with about a dozen men and one woman, and although she didn't end up pursuing anything with the woman, she had a much better time with her. She told the website *Cherwell* that the experience inspired her new song "Femininomenon": "It's about the confusion I have in relation to my sexual relationships with men. Something is not connecting. I feel like every man I've been with is never satisfying. With a woman, it's easy and different and wonderful. It's a phenomenon. It's a queer song–hidden in there . . . It's a phenomenon that this magical, perfect scenario somewhere out there exists, and it's probably a woman in my case."

PREVIOUS
Chappell attends the 67th Grammy Awards on February 2, 2024.

> *"It's a phenomenon that this magical, perfect scenario somewhere out there exists, and it's probably a woman in my case."*

The queerness in "Femininomenon" was a lot less hidden than she thought, yet in "Naked in Manhattan," the lesbian overtones were crystal clear. Sung to a friend she hopes to take things to the next level with, the song explicitly speaks to having sex with a woman for the first time. Chappell later told *NME*, "I was so scared [to go there with a woman] that I wrote a song about it instead."

But something interesting started to happen as the West Hollywood community, and gay men at large, embraced her music. She started to identify as queer. "I think that the project has allowed me to be a part of the queer community in a deeper way because I'm not observing from the outside anymore," she told *Vanity Fair*. "I feel like I'm in it. I am the queer community—it's allowed me to just feel like a queer person and feel freedom in that. It's allowed me to feel safe on stage with the audience because I know a lot of people in the audience are queer and they just want to be there and have a good time."

Stemming from her childhood, there was a lot of internalized shame to get over before she could embrace herself as openly as gay men embraced Chappell. She later told *Qburgh*, "I didn't see myself as queer growing up at all. So that was one thing, one hump I had to go over.

The other hump was loving myself, feeling confident in my body, and loving my music." As she was getting closer to having all three, she was also falling in love with a close friend–a woman. After they shared a kiss on the dance floor, Chappell decided to confront her with her feelings. "[I] told my friend that I was in love with her," she recalled later about the pivotal moment. "She was like, 'Can you just give me a day to think about this?'"

Chappell said yes, but felt racked with anxiety about what her crush might say. So, she did the thing she knew how to do: She sat down and wrote a love song. Ultimately, the friend told her she didn't feel the same, and Chappell was left with a rejection, the ballad "Kaleidoscope," and a new understanding of her sexuality. "I'm so grateful that that happened," she reflected, "because–one–for the first time, I got confirmation that yeah, I am not a fraud for saying that I'm gay. And two–what an incredible person to fall in love with for the first time: your best friend that you think is awesome and hilarious. It was just perfect looking back." They had to take a break from their friendship for a while, but with enough time and space, they found their way back and rekindled their friendship. "I think that's the beautiful thing about the relationships of women," Chappell concluded, "that you can grow up." "Kaleidoscope" became her favorite song she had ever written.

"I feel like I'm in it. I am the queer community—it's allowed me to just feel like a queer person and feel freedom in that."

Party on the Bowery

Thanks to her Sony Publishing deal, Chappell was finally able to quit her job at Donut Friend. When her shows were booked at clubs in Southern California, they all sold out. People often showed up wearing tassel jackets, or glittery cowboy hats, or outrageous costumes like the ones she wore on the covers of her singles—which were all shots to pull inspiration from.

On the cover of "Naked in Manhattan," Chappell is photographed on an outdoor subway platform wearing roller blades and a feathery skirt. For "Casual," Ryan took a photo of her wearing pink fishnets while sitting in the passenger seat of a car, holding a flip phone and drinking what looks like a Mountain Dew Baja Blast. And for "Femininomenon," they went all out: Chappell bedazzled a tracksuit—and her father's dirt bike. Ryan also shot footage of her riding said sparkly bike around the farm that they later played behind her at shows when singing the song.

Chappell loved performing her new music. After waiting two and a half years to sing "Pink Pony Club" live, when she finally did, she wasn't disappointed. "I had no idea the impact of the song until I felt it live," she said on the *Rocket Hour* podcast. She was having more fun than ever on stage, and her audience could feel it. In August, Emily Treadgold wrote in *Earmilk*, "For an artist who has been working for so long, it definitely feels

> *"It's been quite a journey, but I feel like I'm in the best spot I've ever been in … This year has been the most exciting year in my career, and I feel like it's only going to get more exciting."*

like this is the year of Chappell Roan," and quoted her as saying, "It's been quite a journey, but I feel like I'm in the best spot I've ever been in … This year has been the most exciting year in my career, and I feel like it's only going to get more exciting."

That same week, she played the Bowery Ballroom in New York, a legendary venue that's a favorite among upstart and seasoned musicians alike. Everyone was shocked when the tickets sold out, even though she was an independent artist with no label. Years later, she'd tell *Interview* magazine that she felt like she had peaked at that moment. "Back then, I was like, 'I sold out Bowery Ballroom and that's crazy.'"

Even though it's in a dimly lit basement, the Bowery Ballroom is a place to see and be seen, and Chappell's concert was no exception. Chappell had been taking more and more meetings with record labels, while Dan had been brewing up something in the background. With the backing of two colleagues, Justin Eshak and Imran Majid, he was looking into launching a label himself, with Chappell as his first artist.

Justin had never heard her live, so he attended her Bowery show and took Imran with him. "It felt like the walls were gonna rip open," Imran remembered, speaking to *Hits Daily Double*. Justin elaborated, "We went

on a Saturday night and it was [freaking] bonkers. People were losing their minds. Imran and I were like, 'If we can take what's happening right here at Bowery and bring that story to the world, this is going to work.'"

For those who were there, they could attest that the venue wasn't just crowded; the audience *felt* different somehow. "The place was mobbed, but it was so different from things that just had a viral moment," Justin told the *Los Angeles Times*. "This felt old-school in a way that was rooted in a subculture, where everyone there seemed like they were in on something." People dressed up, they sang along; even Olivia showed up. Dan would later tell *Billboard*, "The fact that she's so phenomenal live means people are finally able to see in real time how good she is. That then becomes this word-of-mouth thing, and it's wonderful to see her have such old-school success. I've told so many people, 'This is the way things used to be—you would have to see the artist live, and you see them be good at what they do and then spread the word.'" At the Bowery Ballroom that night, things felt the way they used to be, in the most magical of ways.

Chappell performs at the 2024 Austin City Limits Music Festival in a leather getup and makeup inspired by drag.

FOLLOWING
Chappell performing at weekend two, day three of the Austin City Limits Music Festival on October 13.

"The fact that she's so phenomenal live means people are finally able to see in real time how good she is," Dan told **Billboard**.

The Empowered Redhead

That fall, Chappell embarked on the Girl of My Dreams Tour, opening for queer singer Fletcher. She and Misha set about making costumes, including bedazzled Skechers for Chappell and a shirt covered in Gushers candy for her drummer. Everything was from a thrift store, and she worked hard to incorporate the Midwest aesthetic she grew up with. She later told *Paper*, "Truly, I am not trying to be a chic [girl]. I love the chic [girls], but I am not trying to be like that. Nothing turns me off more than frickin' luxury brands. I feel like, at least where I grew up, Victoria's Secret was a luxury brand. I'm not kidding, that's luxury. Like, Miss Me Jeans. I feel like it comes out in my fashion."

She had no qualms with provocative clothing as she wore clothes that showed off her breasts, butt, thighs, and other physical assets. She did it with purpose. As she told *Cherwell* that summer: "I grew up in a heavily religious, conservative area. The Midwest loves award shows—*American Idol*, we fuel *America's Got Talent*. It creates an 'us' and 'them' mentality—a conversation of 'why do they have to be so slutty? Why can't pop stars just be modest? They don't have to show all that skin.' As a woman, I am allowed to look sexy, and sexualize myself, and feel like a sexual being, taking power in my body. I have no control or power over how others perceive me. I know my grandparents tell me that my voice is good enough, and I don't have to wear what I do. It's almost an act of defiance to be in something very burlesque with nipple tassels, purposely drawing attention to my body. I can be in this outfit and still write a [really] good song and be a good singer. That feels empowering. As long as women feel empowered, then why the [heck] does anyone care what they're wearing? No one's out there asking [Justin] Bieber, 'How does your fashion move feminism forward?'"

As anyone who saw her shows could attest, being unafraid to show herself off is one of the things that made her such a great performer.

When *Cherwell* asked her what she was most looking forward to on tour with Fletcher, she responded, "I love touring. I like how hard it is. The shows are the most exciting part, but they are only 30 percent of the tour. I haven't toured since 2018! Just performing, that is what I'm most excited about." And that's just what she did, playing twenty sold-out shows in major cities including Atlanta, Philadelphia, Montreal, Minneapolis, and Seattle. In New York, her costume ripped, but she kept it from completely falling down and finished the show anyway. In Portland, one afternoon between shows, she decided to dye her hair. "I flew in and we got lunch and you were brunette," Misha recalled later on TikTok. "And then, and then—!" Suddenly, Chappell Roan was forever known as a redhead.

By February 2023, Chappell was finally ready to embark on her first-ever headline tour. They called it "Naked in North America" and booked a month of performances at the most respected midsized theaters in the country.

Before the tour, she and her team came up with themes for each show, giving her fans opportunities to dress up with her. "That's the whole point of the tour: to give people a safe space to come and dress up," she told *Nylon*. "No one's going to say anything mean to you. And you

Chappell's Influences

Burlesque

Burlesque is one of the oldest forms of entertainment in the United States, a cousin of vaudeville and variety shows. Famous old-time comedians Abbott & Costello and Phil Silvers got their start in burlesque, and in the olden days, burlesque shows would contain all kinds of performers--the only rule was that it should be racier and less family-friendly than vaudeville.

However, the burlesque striptease had its roots in feminism. While shows like *Ziegfeld Follies* featured homogenized "all-American girls" with a slender look, burlesque featured more varied body types. *Follies* girls were hand-selected by Ziegfeld to stand bare-breasted in front of his audiences. But women working in burlesque, like star Gypsy Rose Lee, removed their clothes themselves, which was seen as risqué. Burlesque also catered to a more working-class audience, playing into ideas about how social status affects perception of female bodies. "I want to purposely look 'trashy,' not modest; very loud and provocative. To me that is a reflection of and an homage to burlesque," Chappell told *Cherwell*.

In today's day and age, burlesque lives on almost exclusively as women performers who wear elaborate yet revealing outfits and perform physically demanding dances many would consider to be erotic. Their incredible showmanship is always reflected in their costumes. As Chappell put it simply to *Vulture*, "I love burlesque outfits because they're so dramatic and pretty and sparkly and intricate."

Natalie Wood stars as Gyspy Rose Lee in the 1962 musical-drama movie, *Gypsy*.

can dance and be queer." In Dallas and Denver, the theme was "Drag & Disco"; in Houston, Washington, and Columbus, it was "Rhinestones & Rainbows." Philadelphia got "Goth, Grunge & Glitter," while Salt Lake City dressed up to "Slumber Party Kissin'." In New York, the theme would be "So You Wanna Be a Popstar," and while all her other outfits were thrifted, Chappell commissioned this one—a Hannah Montana dress, and not just any Hannah Montana dress. "I went out to the fabric district in LA [and] searched for hours for the fabric I wanted," she told the style magazine. "I specifically wanted to copy a Hannah Montana look that I saw when I saw the Jonas Brothers open for her in Kansas City in 2008."

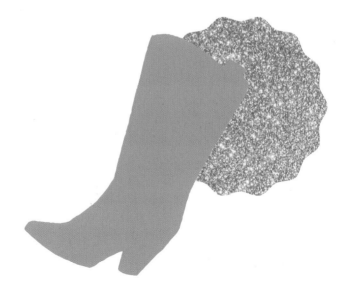

"That's the whole point of the tour: to give people a safe space to come and dress up... And you can dance and be queer."

Getting Hot (to Go)

Finally old enough to drive a rented van, Chappell drove from city to city towing a U-Haul trailer, curating costumes for herself and her all-girl backup band, and doing whatever publicity she could drum up for herself. Before her first show, in Phoenix, Arizona, she talked to news company Pop Crave, who asked if there was a song she was most excited to perform live. She responded, "It's a new one! It's called 'HOT TO GO!' I wrote it just a couple weeks ago, and it is a cheer song, so there's a dance attached to it that I teach the audience. It's fun!"

Sung in the style of a cheerleading chant, "HOT TO GO!" was inspired by Queen's audience-participation-fueled performance at the 1985 Live Aid concert—which Chappell had seen in the movie *Bohemian Rhapsody*, then in a YouTube video. "The whole crowd was doing this thing," she told *Teen Vogue*, who caught up with her in early March. "I was like, how do I make the crowd do that?"

During the Naked in North America Tour, she led the crowd through spelling out H-O-T-T-O-G-O in a reimagined Y-M-C-A. Now, not only could everyone have a safe space to dress up and not feel silly, they could dress up while they were doing it. Picking out someone and forcing them to do the dance also became a staple of her show.

In a story to *QBurgh*, she said, "Last night I played Salt Lake City [Utah]. Obviously, everyone's dressed up, there's drag queens in the crowd. There's a lot of twinky girlies and there's the occasional random straight boyfriend standing right front and center, just there for his girlfriend. And it's every show. Everywhere I play there's always just one random boy who doesn't want to be there, but it's fine. They're the ones I pick on the whole time. I called some guy out last night and I was like . . . 'Are you good at dancing?' And he was like, 'No.' I was like, 'Well, we are about to teach you "HOT TO GO!"' He was very embarrassed. I could tell he hated it, but I was like, 'You're at my show. You're going to have fun.'"

Making sure everyone had fun—even the random straight guys—was what Chappell loved most about performing. "It's a dream come true," she later told Sam Prance. "The only thing I want to offer as a human is to make a space where there is joy where there wasn't before. That is like magic: to be able to walk into a room that was empty, and there were no feelings, and now there are feelings of happiness. I don't think there is anything I could ever want more than that, that's the dream come true. There's literally nothing else better than that."

Chappell's dedication to making a magical experience for her audience was apparent to everyone who attended one of her shows. "The nightly concepts may differ, but the underlying theme of these shows is the same," *Teen Vogue* wrote, "this is a place for queer joy, for feeling yourself, for the cathartic release of fear and anxiety in one shining dancefloor moment."

"You're at my show. You're going to have fun."

One way she set the jubilant mood before she even hit the stage was in her choice of opening acts. In each city, she hired local drag acts to perform. With their beautiful and intricate outfits, sassy attitudes, and charisma with the crowd, they fired up fans who were both super-familiar with drag and those who had never seen a drag performer live.

Showing her support for the drag community did more than help widen their fan base and put some extra tips in their pockets. Yet, on February 23, the very day when she was playing Nashville with the queens Cya Inhale, Delta Granta, and Alexia Noelle Paris, Tennessee lawmakers passed a bill that made it illegal for drag queens to perform on public property or in venues that didn't enforce age restrictions. It was the first state to pass such a law, but it wouldn't be the last.

The sponsor of the bill, representative Chris Todd, had called a recent drag show "child abuse." In *Teen Vogue*, Chappell vehemently disagreed. "[The bill is] not about kids, it's about attacking trans people," she told them. To her, and many in the community, passing that bill was "a lot more about harassing trans people, or people who wanna dress how they wanna dress. It comes from a lot of fear and a lot of confusion and hatred."

Chappell wanted to speak out publicly against the law, but she didn't want to put the performers who were opening for her at risk from bigots, including bigots who could put her in jail. Instead, she complied with the age restrictions, hired extra security for her Nashville show, and her other shows in the South, and donated a portion of her tour proceeds to a trans charity called For the Gworls. Most of all, she tried to show the world what drag really was. "It's devastating," she later told Sam Prance. "I've performed in pretty much all the places that it's banned, and you can feel it with the queens, the heaviness in the room. I think it's really

"To be able to walk into a room that was empty, and there were no feelings, and now there are feelings of happiness. I don't think there is anything I could ever want more than that."

> "I think it's most important to give those queens and kings a platform and just show the world that this is joy, it isnt whatever the [heck] you think it is."

important, especially in those places, to keep drag alive ... drag isn't going anywhere ... I think it's most important to give those queens and kings a platform and just show the world that this is joy, it isn't whatever the [heck] you think it is."

In New York, after drag queens Jamie CD, Sasha Vanguard, and Christine Dior performed, Chappell and her backing band took the stage as some of their favorite pop stars: Lana Del Rey, Avril Lavigne, David Bowie, and–of course–Hannah Montana. Chappell started the show in a blonde wig, but after the third song of the set, she removed it while audio from *Hannah Montana* played over the speakers: Miley telling her friend Lily "I'm Hannah Montana," while she removes her own wig. Chappell took off her wig, revealing her blazing red hair, and continued the show. When she did one of her favorite covers, Alanis Morissette's "You Oughta Know," the crowd went wild. She did her usual encore, "Pink Pony Club," and confetti cannons pelted the audience. As she danced off the stage, she blew kisses to the crowd.

Chappell on the Midwest Princess Tour at FirstBank Ampitheater in Franklin, Tennessee, on October 1, 2024.

"Rising Star Chappell Roan Meets Her Moment with Ecstatic New York Show" the headline read the next day in *Variety*, which wrote, "She's a powerful singer and a masterful performer, with practiced strutting and hair-flips and emphatic punches, and she knows how to pace her show . . . The audience isn't just singing along with the hit but with nearly every song, half of them with hands over hearts, many dressed in the artist's merch or artist-identifying outfits, and at least a few singing emphatically, with tears and/or mascara running . . . A superstar is born? On the basis of Tuesday night, Chappell Roan already was one—it's just taken the world a minute to catch up."

She had won over the sophisticated New York crowd, but she had a show coming up that she was even more nervous about: her hometown. She was playing the Gillioz Theatre in Springfield, and she wasn't sure she had enough fans there to sell out the one thousand seats. The theme they had picked was "Homecoming Queen." Could she follow through?

Chappell's Homecoming

After playing New York, Chappell performed in Boston, Toronto, Columbus, and Chicago, until finally taking the stage in Springfield. She had accomplished an incredible amount since working at the coffee kiosk: she'd recorded numerous new songs, headlined her own tour, and established a rabid fanbase. No longer was she a struggling artist trying to find her sound. But even with all the success, in her hometown, Chappell still felt like the same Kayleigh Rose who never fit in. Sure, she could sell out the Bowery Ballroom in New York, but what about the Gillioz Theatre in Springfield?

Her first surprise was that the venue had sold out. Her second was that they had sold to total strangers—people who had grown up in the same place as her who she had never known. "I looked out and I thought I would recognize everyone, and I hardly saw anyone I knew!" she said later on in a documentary shot by Jackie!. "And for the first time ever, the wall—the fear of me not belonging in my hometown—was broken by knowing that there are so many queer people here." When she looked up from singing one of her new ballads, "Coffee," the crowd had turned on their cell phone flashlights and were swaying with her. She felt so accepted, she cried. Afterwards, some fans thanked her for creating a safe community in Springfield for queer people.

When the US tour was finally over, she gave one last interview, to a student-run paper at the University of Southern California. When they congratulated her on finishing her tour and asked how she felt, she replied, "I feel really tired. But it's a good tired. I loved it. It was just so [frickin'] hard. The shows, the queens, and the band, they made it all worth it." When asked her favorite moment, she replied, "My hometown, probably. I've never played my hometown. And I've never asked the crowd to put up flashlights on their phones or whatever, but they did... It gave me a new appreciation and love for my hometown, which I really struggle with, because I did not have a good time growing up. There's a community here for me, and I never knew that existed before then. It was really special."

But something even more special was about to come: her first full-length album. A culmination of more than three years of work, it would be the album that would change everything.

Chappell takes the stage at the Brixton Academy theater in London, UK, on September 21, 2024, during her Midwest Princess Tour.

"For the first time ever, the wall—the fear of me not belonging in my hometown—was broken by knowing that there are so many queer people here."

A Good Deal

Chappell couldn't call her new album "Femininomenon" because even she had trouble saying it correctly. So she went with another phrase that had been ringing around her head: Midwest Princess. "I posted in 2022 the title, and I didn't even know the album was going to exist yet," she told Jackie!. "It just all made sense—I got a tramp stamp that literally says 'Princess' and I was like, 'Oh this all makes sense, this works, all of it works.'"

The album, whose full name would incorporate the famous epithet "The Rise and Fall" to become *The Rise and Fall of a Midwest Princess*, included fourteen tracks. Kayleigh Amstutz received solo writing credit for "Kaleidoscope," but she and Dan shared dual credit on "Femininomenon," "HOT TO GO!", and a ballad called "Picture You." They also included "California" and "Pink Pony Club," which Atlantic had given them the rights to. Eight of the other songs were made even better by bringing in more collaborators—Dan always felt that "you have to service the song." He told *Music Business Worldwide*, "If it takes four songwriters to make a song, amazing, it takes four. If it takes six, it takes six. If it takes only two, great." Sometimes, they also brought in extra producers. For "Red Wine Supernova," an innuendo-filled anthem with a soaring chorus, they brought in three extra writers, including the singers Annie Schindel and AMES. "I remember when we finally nailed the song, my body was tingling," Dan recalled to *The Washington Post*. "I'd run home and play it for my wife."

Finally, Chappell had a whole album of songs, but she didn't have a label. The truth was, "you can only go so far as an independent artist," she told Adam Lisicky. "I don't have $50,000 to go do a tour with. I need a label for that kind of stuff." Dan had become more and more interested in the business side of the music industry, and, he later told *Fast Company*, "I wanted nothing more than for people to listen to Chappell."

Justin Eshak and Imran Majid had just taken over a struggling label owned by Universal Music Group, Island Records, and the three of them saw a mutually beneficial deal: Dan launched Amusement Records, an imprint backed by Island. His first and only artist was Chappell Roan. "I was so in love with everything that we were doing," Dan told *Billboard*. "I just believe in [Chappell] so much that I was like, 'Do I want this added stress in my life? Is it worth it?' And the answer was, 'Yes.'"

*"I wanted nothing more than for people to listen to Chappell," Dan told **Fast Company**.*

Instead of getting a terrible deal like Atlantic had presented her with as a teenager, now "I probably have one of the best deals ever in modern music," she told *The Face,* laughing. "Because I was like, '[Forget] you guys, give me what I want or I'm going to do this myself.'" The deal they asked for granted them complete creative control over *The Rise and Fall of a Midwest Princess*, plus all of its marketing–virtually unheard of in the music business. Dan later recalled to *Hits Daily Double*, "We brought the record to Island and kind of said, 'This is our album. These are the songs we want to release. This is how we want to do it. This is our publicist. This is our creative director. We have the whole package. We just need a partner.'"

From Justin and Imran's point of view, they were the ones getting the great deal. "At that point, Justin and I were the new kids on the block," Imran said. "There wasn't any recent success we could point to. But I think we had the right temperament and understanding." When the contracts were signed, they didn't even make an official announcement. "[Chappell's] new label, Island, has kept things low-key–" *Variety* mused, "so much that they didn't even officially announce her signing: They're letting her and her audience lead."

The Queer-Beauty in the Details

Chappell knew that the best way to lead was to help build the world of Chappell Roan from the ground up. Delving into all aspects of storytelling, she was hands-on when it came to the costumes and sets for her music videos and album art. She and Misha made Pinterest boards, and Chappell watched tutorials on YouTube and did her own hair and makeup. All of her outfits had been bought or sewed (or more often, a combination of the two) by either Chappell or Misha. Sometimes a friend helped with the more complicated pieces, but others were simply thrifted or bought off Etsy.

For three of her music videos, they shot back in her hometown, with her friend Hadley from Interlochen as director. And when the heels broke off her shoes for the "My Kink is Karma" video, she simply glued them back on and kept going. Everyone worked for free or reduced prices.

Ryan shot an epic album cover: Chappell as the Midwest Princess. Wearing a blue gown (with—naturally—a bedazzled trim), a tiara, and a sash with her name spelled out in glitter, Chappell posed in front of a vanity mirror, framed by old-fashioned light bulbs. It was an image that would be everywhere by the end of next summer. Drag queen Trixie Mattel would later joke that it was even better up close. "The album artwork, with the super fair face, and sumptuous, glitter-red lips. Super graphic eyes . . ." she told Chappell in a *Paper* interview, "when you played

Chappell's Collaborators

For Chappell, finding the right collaborators makes all the difference. "There's a really good language between us when it comes to making music," Dan Nigro, her longtime producer and writing partner, told *Billboard*. "She's so good at explaining exactly what she wants, and it makes for a really good flow."

Chappell's collaborations go far beyond writing. She works with stylists, agents, publicists, managers, assistants, audio engineers, a live music director, and--of course--other musicians. "She cares a lot about cultivating a really good environment," her drummer, Lucy Ritter, told Iowa Public Radio. Chappell's collaborators don't have to share the same background or style as her, but she does seek out the best. When she wanted to perfect the sound on "Super Graphic Ultra Modern Girl," she contacted Charli XCX's producer Mike Weiss. When she saw a video of Miley Cyrus warming up her vocal chords, she hired her vocal coach. But one of her favorite collaborators might be Ramisha Sattar, who she reached out to on Instagram after admiring her art. She now counts Misha as both her creative director and her best friend.

on TV, and I could see your face blown up, I'd get in there and look, like, 'This [diva] is painted out of her mind.'" From a drag queen, it was a true compliment.

Misha and Chappell wanted to make the vinyl album even more special, so they met in a coffee shop to brainstorm. "We want[ed] it to feel like those old story books that pop out, or just vintage Victorian stationery where there's so much hand detailing, which obviously is hard to do when you're mass producing something," Misha told *Creative Independent*. "It's hard to get the handmade feel." What they came up with, as they sketched out some ideas at the café, was a theater stage as the frame of the vinyl. Later, they'd even release Chappell-inspired paper dolls that Misha drew herself.

The delight in details, storytelling, and world-building was especially apparent in the music videos they created. In "Red Wine Supernova," Chappell courts a female magician, and their love story is punctuated with a nosy neighbor who affects the perfect scowl while she watches them flirt. (Later, she plants a campy "God Hates Magic" sign on the front lawn.) In the video for "Casual," it's a mermaid Chappell is after, and the bedroom she brings her home to looks straight out of a '90s dream, with the same pink and light-green palette as the album cover, a crocheted flower blanket, and magazine photos taped to the wall. In the video, Chappell works to make it comfortable for her girlfriend–changing the pink to sea blue, adding an eel mobile, and creating a campy "welcome home" sign out of shells. But her mermaid-girlfriend rejects her, so she destroys the whole thing. The amount of homemade details are incredible–there's even a beret bedazzled in shells.

In "Naked in Manhattan," shot by Ryan, she's seen (still with brown hair) running around New York City, jumping off construction barricades, and singing next to a row of Citi Bikes in a ruffled red dress. For "HOT TO GO!", she dances her way around Springfield and Willard for a video that Jackie! shot, including locations at a gas station, a mini-golf course, the Gillioz Theatre, and in front of her grandparents' house. (They gamely spell out "Hot to Go" with their arms, along with her.)

In "My Kink is Karma," a song about a breakup cowritten by Justin Tranter, Chappell is seen decorating a cake, Rollerblading down the street, straddling a clown (while she's also in clown makeup), eating a Cheeto in a hot tub full of rubber ducks, and, rather iconically, sitting in a pile of her own belongings on the lawn crying, while her makeup runs down her face.

In all the videos, the details—an '80s-era portable television, a landline phone shaped like a high-heeled shoe, a half-eaten bologna and cheese sandwich in front of a picture of Jesus—are worthy of a Wes Anderson film, more thought-out than a major label could ever muster. "I've never been so in love with art that I've made," Chappell told drag queen Mo Heart.

TRACK 4

STAGE PRINCESS

"Dude, I have four weeks until the [stuff] hits the fan," Chappell told a reporter from *Vanity Fair* a month before *The Rise and Fall of a Midwest Princess* released. By this point, she was getting more and more attention from journalists, who were always interested in unique personalities on the brink of popularity. In addition to appearing in *Variety* and *Vanity Fair*, in 2023 Chappell appeared in culture and style mainstays *Rolling Stone*, *Vogue*, *Nylon*, *V*, *Pitchfork*, *Vulture*, and the *Los Angeles Times*. *The Washington Post* also devoted a feature to her in their Style section with the headline "Chappell Roan doesn't care if she's going to hell."

Of course, Chappell had been giving interviews for more than six years at this point. In 2017, the *Springfield News-Leader* wrote, "Her speaking voice is a typical teenager's, with the added poise of someone learning to answer frequent questions from interviewers." By late 2022, *Rolling Stone* had interviewed her, and used Chappell's own words to describe her style—"thrift store pop"—right in their headline. In 2023, *Pitchfork* was writing, "Within 10 minutes of our initial meeting, Roan has already prompted me to Google 'Azealia Banks chicken slaughter' (terrifying, fascinating) and registered to become an ordained minister online, so one day she can officiate a wedding in Las Vegas as a possible ticket-boosting stunt. Later, she pulls down the band of her skirt to reveal a tramp stamp that reads 'Princess.'"

Not only was she good at entertaining reporters and giving quotable sound bites, she spoke candidly. When *Vanity Fair* asked her if she was surprised by her growing popularity, she responded, "Not to be

PREVIOUS
Chappell at the 2024 MTV Video Music Awards on September 11.

FOLLOWING
Chappell winning Best New Artist at the MTV Video Music Awards in Elmont, New York.

> *"I'm not surprised that it's still going so well... It's just very validating to be like, oh, my gut was right."*

[arrogant], but I'm not surprised. I'm not surprised that it's still going so well... It's just very validating to be like, oh, my gut was right." She did admit, however, to being ecstatic over the news that the store Urban Outfitters was going to be carrying her vinyl. "That's a big deal for sixteen-year-old me," she said. "Like, that's crazy. But everything else I'm just like, 'yeah.'"

Chappell wasn't surprised she was getting popular, but she still hadn't gotten used to fans coming up to her in public. In the moment, she'd smile, and take a few selfies, but it was beginning to feel more and more strange to be recognized. Olivia Rodrigo seemed to handle it so well. "She's so good at being a normal person when everything is abnormal around her," Chappell told *Nylon*. "I don't feel like a normal person right now, and I'm not even near where she is." She asked Olivia how she dealt with fame, but Olivia didn't know what to tell her. "She was like, 'I don't have the answers, I'm sorry. No one has the answers.'"

Although Chappell's encroaching fame felt weird, personally Kayleigh was doing better than ever. She was in her first lesbian relationship, which she described to *Nylon* as "happy and healthy." She had finally started watching *RuPaul's Drag Race*. And best of all, she had finally found meds for her bipolar II disorder that were working well for her. She was starting to feel better. As she explained to the *Daily Trojan*, "Being bipolar, I was so depressed as a little kid and so angry. You just think you're such a

"Actually, you're a good person, and you're creating a safe space and music for people to dance to."

bad person, and don't realize that you're really sick and need help. I think it's like rewiring my brain to be like, 'Actually, you're a good person, and you're creating a safe space and music for people to dance to.'"

And she was about to do just that in a major way, by headlining a new tour in support of her album—and this time, on a bus. "I am so excited," she told *Vanity Fair*. "I've never done a bus tour. I've never been able to afford it, but I can and that's a game changer . . . If it wasn't so dangerous, I would literally wrap the bus in something like, [super] crazy. But it's just so dangerous 'cause people know where you are. I am just so excited. I am just so excited. I love touring."

Three days before the tour began, on September 22, 2023, Chappell's first full-length album was released. Chappell wrote on Instagram: "This album is for the ten-year-old girl from the Midwest who never thought she could be herself. The girl who felt shame from the day she turned thirteen for having a deeper love for her girl best friend that was unlike anything she felt for boys. For the girl who was told to be proper and sweet and ladylike, but simply would never be.

"I hope you feel freedom and joy when you listen. I hope it gives you solace in the difficult times.

"My dreams have already come true because I have seen the joy this music has created out of thin air. That's all I can ever ask for. I am proud of myself for daring to fail, and yet against all obstacles, succeeding."

Chappell performs for thousands while opening for Olivia Rodrigo at the Acrisure Arena in Palm Springs, California, in February 2024.

"We did it <3."

The critics adored it. *Rolling Stone* said, "Chappell Roan is a wildly ribald, extremely hooky thrill ride through sexual and personal awakenings." *Pitchfork* called it "a bold and uproarious introduction, buoyed by sturdy songcraft and steely indifference of good taste." *NME* called her an "ascendant star" and—although it liked the pop songs more than the ballads—it called the album "a display of Roan's bold and brazen pen, where she places searing revelations alongside some deliciously cheeky choruses." At the end of the year, it appeared on "The Best of 2023" lists at *Rolling Stone*, *Billboard*, and *Vogue*. *Time*, which named it the fourth best album of the year, called her "the pop heroine America needs." Amazon Music named her the Breakout Artist of the Year and plastered an enormous poster of her on the side of a building in Brooklyn.

Maybe it was because the album was entirely independently made, maybe it was because Chappell had spent so long honing her persona, or maybe it was simply her natural charisma and singing ability—whatever it was, critics heard it. *The Rise and Fall of a Midwest Princess* was the rarest of things in pop music: It was original. *Paper* writer Joan Summers said her sound countered "frictionless, easy-going pop music, sanded down by glittering synths and chic outfits and the sameness of auto-generated Spotify playlists." At the same time, Kate Solomon from *The Guardian* credited her with a new shift in the entire genre, saying, "Pop had been in a dark place since the mid-2010s: mumbled confessions over seething beats and sparse bedroom laments. But Roan is an explosion of color."

> *"Pop had been in a dark place since the mid-2010s... But Roan is an explosion of color," said* **The Guardian**.

Queer reviewers were ecstatic. "That [Chappell] is reaching back to the buried queerness of YMCA and linking past with present for a throughline that brings our queer stories full circle suggests this moment isn't just a flash in the pan. She's gathering us around a rallying cry of authenticity that has been absent from pop culture in recent memory," wrote Roger Porter on *EDGE*.

Unfortunately, while critics praised it, and her fans couldn't have been more excited, the album wasn't hitting the kinds of streaming numbers other top artists were getting—at least, not at first. I used to say her fan base was not as wide, but it was very deep," Kiely Mosiman, one of her agents, recalled to the *Times*. "Like, if you listen to Chappell Roan, you're a huge fan of Chappell Roan." It was true: She had built a solid fan base, but she still didn't have the mainstream recognition to crack the *Billboard* 200. But Chappell didn't care about charts—she was more focused on her tour than on her numbers.

"After this album comes out, what do you see as the next big step in your career?" *Vulture* asked her. "There's a few things that I want to do," Chappell responded. "I want to sell out the fall tour. And I want to do a UK tour next spring. But that's kind of it. I just love touring. The only Grammy I want to win is album packaging. My best friend [Misha] and I, we saw all the nominations for packaging for the past ten years and were like, 'Oh, we've got this in the bag.' And we've been doing spells and manifestations to see if it works to win us a Grammy. But that's it. I'm just trying to have fun."

FOLLOWING
Chappell performing on her Midwest Princess Tour at the Brixton Academy in London, England, on September 19, 2024.

"I want to sell out the fall tour. And I want to do a UK tour next spring. But that's kind of it. I just love touring."

The Tour of a Princess

The first stop of the Midwest Princess Tour was Chappell's return to the Gillioz Theatre in Springfield. Like every other venue she played on the thirty-four–show tour, it sold out. Traveling across the US and Canada in her fancy tour bus, she went from Denver to Nashville to Toronto to New York—and after that, she still had two weeks to go.

"I love touring. It's my favorite part of my job, which is very rare and most people [really] hate it," she told *Vanity Fair*. It was even one of the reasons Dan had transitioned from being a frontman into being a producer, as he told *Music Business Worldwide*: "I found myself quite disconnected from reality at some points. You're living in this weird alternate bubble, where you're moving around, going from show to show, you're in a new city, you show up at a venue, you're performing and then . . . doing it all over again." But for Chappell, it provided a sense of calm.

Even though it was often exhausting, she could focus on her tour with few other distractions, and knew she was exactly where she wanted to be. She told *Qburgh*, "I feel really at peace, which is something that I didn't really know I would feel. But I just feel gratitude and peace . . . I'm proud that I kept going through all of the part-time jobs, through being dropped by a label, through all the breakups, through all the times my bank account was nearly empty . . . as long as I'm literally putting on shows that make people happy or playing music that makes people feel seen

> "As long as I'm literally putting on shows that make people happy or playing music that makes people feel seen and heard, I can't ask for anything else. All my dreams came true. This is it; I don't need anything else."

and heard, I can't ask for anything else. All my dreams came true. This is it; I don't need anything else."

Critics seemed especially impressed when Chappell sold out the New York venue Brooklyn Steel, which had an 1,800-patron capacity–and not just for one night, but for two. "My Chappell Roan concert experience begins as I exit the subway," a reviewer wrote in *Document*. "Young women walk Grand Street in holographic cowboy boots paired with sequined dresses, sporting glitter on their eyes and shoulders." Tipped off by queer actor Bowen Yang (who was there both nights), the talent bookers from *Saturday Night Live* even came to take a look.

In LA, where the theme was "My Kink is Karma," *Rolling Stone* reported that "pink plastic cows and fake aqua-blue trucks decorated the lobby of the Wiltern. Her fans–donning sparkly devil horns and bedazzled bralettes decorated with hearts–posed for photos in front of the backdrops."

The *Barbie* movie had been released a few months prior, and pink cowboy hats proliferated. Many fans held homemade signs (or sometimes, for a "Femininomenon" reference, just a Papa John's pizza box). While she sang "Kaleidoscope," it became an audience custom to hold colored tissue paper over their phone flashlights. They also started making homemade bracelets out of colored thread, also known as friendship bracelets, and would trade them with new friends they made at the show.

Chappell once again set the scene by inviting local drag performers to be her openers. In Vancouver, reviewer V. S. Wells wrote, "It's a smart move: nobody screams more than a room full of [excited] patrons seeing a stunt queen do splits and dips." At the end of their act, the drag performers awarded a crown and sash to their pick for the best-dressed audience member, in this case, a fan with a "flawless pink-and-green mine-faced aesthetic." And then Chappell took the stage and brought down the house. Wells continued, "The party starts in earnest when Roan takes the stage, backed by a three-femme band . . . clad in oversized bikini-print tees and holographic visors; the singer herself shimmies in a superhero-esque lamé two-piece, wreathed in rainbow flowers. Kicking off with album opener 'Femininomenon,' Roan's vocals are both rawer and stronger live . . . [During the encore], cowboy hats go flying. The volume cranks. "Pink Pony Club" starts up, and there's no containing the sweaty, shouting, exuberant mess that the standing room becomes."

"Nobody screams more than a room full of [excited] patrons seeing a stunt queen do splits and dips," said reporter Wells.

At each show, Chappell played almost every song off her new album. For most shows, she also threw in a cover of Lady Gaga's "Bad Romance." And in some cities, she played a song fans weren't so familiar with–one of her earlier tunes like "Bitter," "Good Hurt," or "School Nights." Even though she no longer connected with those songs, she wanted to honor her younger self. In front of such big crowds, "Sixteen-year-old me would have died to play those songs," she told Sam Prance at *Capital Buzz*.

In November and December 2023, she would finally bring her tour abroad to Australia and Europe, including two nights in London. But while that might've been her biggest dream of the year, the venue that twenty-five-year-old Chappell was most excited about playing was Heaven, in London–the legendary gay club once frequented by Freddie Mercury and numerous other icons. She sold out Heaven both nights. "That was so affirming for me because Heaven is famously so joyous," she told British music magazine *NME*. It was more unusual than it seemed: A pop icon for gay men who is also an out lesbian is simply something the world had never seen before.

FOLLOWING
Chappell onstage at Austin City Limits on October 13, 2024.

When Chappell sold out both nights at Heaven, she said, "That was so affirming for me because Heaven is famously so joyous."

Big Arenas and One Tiny Desk

In early 2024, Chappell got an incredible opportunity to expand her fan base when Olivia Rodrigo invited her to be an opener on her Guts Tour. They were a good pair to be reckoned with: "The two don't just share a producer but a bratty spirit," *Billboard* wrote. On Olivia's tour, Chappell would be playing the biggest venues of her career, but mostly in midsized cities and for audiences who might not have heard of her. It just might've been the move she needed to finally obtain mainstream recognition.

On X, Chappell began trending for the first time. "Oh my god oh my god oh my godddd I AM SO EXCITED," she wrote on Instagram. To *NME* she confessed, "I'm just not really sure how it's gonna feel to do an arena show!" They played twenty-four cities, including Austin, Orlando, and St. Louis. "It's different but not that different," she told *Rolling Stone*. "There's a lot more younger girls than at my shows, but the best audience ever is teenage girls." In addition to opening for Olivia, she also joined her on stage at some shows (including during her Netflix special) to perform "HOT TO GO!" "This just rocks," she told the iconic music magazine. "It's amazing to be living up my little pop-star life. It's so slay."

> "There's a lot more younger girls [at Olivia's shows] than at my shows, but the best audience ever is teenage girls."

In the midst of the tour, she made an appearance that would break open her audience even more—on NPR's *Tiny Desk* concert series. Its cocreator, Stephen Thompson, had been a Chappell fan since 2022, and after the release of *Midwest Princess*, he invited her to NPR's Washington, DC headquarters to do a set on the popular web series. He later recalled to *The Washington Post* that he thought, "If her vocals are as on-point as I think they're going to be, I think she's really going to hit it out of the park." She did.

On the cramped set full of books and knickknacks, she performed five songs backed by a seven-member band—all wearing pink outfits and blue eyeshadow. Chappell's own look was campy, intricate, and flawless. Wearing a poofy, hot-pink Betsey Johnson cocktail dress; a giant, gaudy butterfly pendant; and dark-red press-on nails sharpened into points, she announced between songs, "I didn't really watch the Super Bowl last night . . . This is my Super Bowl."

Her most distinguishing feature, however, was her red beehive wig, festooned with butterfly ornaments and stubbed-out cigarettes. She topped it off with a sparkly flower tiara that let some bangs hang down. By now, she had also started wearing even more dramatic makeup, including painting her whole face white.

Chappell had begun to think of her look as drag. One night before a show in London, she told her opener, a drag queen named Crayola, that she had to go and put on her makeup and transform. When Chappell likened herself to a drag queen, Crayola took it a step further. "She was like, 'Honey, you *are* a drag queen, you're not just getting makeup on, you're a drag queen,'" Chappell recounted to Tom Power on his podcast.

Chappell's Influences

Women Musicians

One of the ways Chappell keeps herself continually inspired is by listening to new music, especially women musicians. "Anything that I listen to—Joan Jett, Heart, Gaga—I want to feel like them. So, I'll just be inspired by that feeling and how I can capture it," she told *Rolling Stone*. Here are some of the singers Chappell has admired over the years.

Pink. "My first CD I ever got was Pink," Chappell recalled to *Refinery29*. "I was in kindergarten. And I just thought she was so cool and just so confident and amazing."

Stevie Nicks. "I really love Stevie Nicks, her gravel and the vibrato she brought," Chappell told the Associated Press about the Fleetwood Mac singer, whom she tried to emulate when she was just starting out.

Lady Gaga. Chappell loved Gaga growing up, and has often cited her as an inspiration for her stage persona, her inclusive ideology, and the audience participation aspects of her music. She's also been known to cover "Bad Romance" in concert.

Sekitō Shigeo. Cited as a current obsession in 2024 to *Rolling Stone*, Sekitō is known as one of the all-time masters of the Electone, a Yamaha electronic organ.

Kate Bush. Chappell told *Vulture* she loves "anthemic pop" like Kate Bush, Cyndi Lauper, and Shania Twain. And when asked by the *Daily Trojan* to describe *The Rise and Fall of a Midwest Princess*, she said, "It's like Kate Bush but a little sluttier. Just a little more queer."

Lady Gaga performing during her Jazz & Piano residency at Park MGM in Las Vegas, Nevada, on October 14, 2021.

"That was the first time I had ever been told that... That was very altering."

"That was the first time I had ever been told that... That was very altering." Drag queen Trixie Mattel later told her, "There's always been this dialogue between pop stars and drag queens. I feel like you're the missing link, because you're part pop star, part drag queen."

Chappell started to paint her face white, inspired by clown makeup and the fact that in Willard, people would sometimes call gay people clowns. "I was just like, '[Girl], I'll show you a clown, if you want to see a clown!'" she told *Paper*. "So I started doing that and also referencing the girls in the '20s, all the classic stuff. Also, my blue eyeshadow, I always love blue eyeshadow and a big red lip; glitter... my faves."

Recently, she had perfected her visual persona even further by hiring a stylist: Genesis Webb. Chappell and Genesis had met the year before on a magazine photo shoot. They were the same age, from the Midwest, and living in LA. Chappell was impressed with her style, especially her knowledge of burlesque and drag. They knew each other only a week before Chappell asked Genesis to become her official stylist, helping Chappell perfect her look and devise costumes for each of her appearances on the Midwest Princess Tour. Genesis's first move was making Chappell upgrade her footwear. Chappell told *The Washington Post* she recalled Genesis telling her, "You can't wear Skechers onstage."

Tiny Desk had the viewership to help launch artists, and Genesis went all out for Chappell's look. She even smoked cigarettes to include in the wig. "At 6 a.m. at the hotel, I was outside like a gremlin, lighting Marlboro Reds, just chain-smoking," she told *British Vogue*. The look was so iconic, the *Tiny Desk* producers asked if they could keep the wig and display it on one of the shelves in the background for all future concerts. (Chappell said yes, and they placed it on top of a skull Cypress Hill gave them.)

Everyone agreed that the set was something special. Chappell had an opportunity to show off her vocal skills, and the band was grouped tightly behind her. When playing large shows, they always had audio earpieces with a click track—a metronome that helped them keep the beat. But at *Tiny Desk*, they were without the extra audio input, just listening to each other and keeping time together. For drummer Lucy Ritter, who had been playing with Chappell since the Midwest Princess tour, it was particularly meaningful. "I've been watching those [*Tiny Desk* concerts] since I was a kid," she told Iowa Public Radio, "and idolizing the performances, idolizing the musicality, you know, thinking about how unrealistic that performance space is and how people make do. Walking into that office and seeing the set—and it's verbatim what I remember in my brain—was really special, and also one of those childhood bucket-list checkmarks."

Another person who was thrilled? Kara Amstutz. "I felt like a big girl pop star," Chappell told *Rolling Stone* about the show. "I don't read comments, so all I really know is that my mom is really excited." The video was posted on March 21 and took off like wildfire. Then, suddenly, so did Chappell: That week, her online streaming numbers made a giant leap from seven million to almost eleven million. The combination of the *Tiny Desk* appearance, the Guts Tour, word of mouth, more and more interviews—and perhaps especially, the coalescing of her Chappell persona—had made Chappell something she had never been before: popular.

"I don't read comments, so all I really know is that my mom is really excited."

Chronically Online

When Chappell started blowing up, a fan posted a video they had taken back in 2021, shortly after Chappell had moved back to LA. It was one of the first times she had performed "Pink Pony Club" publicly, at a nonprofit Pride event with few bells and whistles. In the video, Chappell stands alone behind her keyboard. Her hair is still brown, she's hardly wearing any makeup, and her outfit–though it's red–is downright drab by her later standards. Her white sneakers aren't even bedazzled. Yet, she's giving it the same heart, belting out the same "Pink Pony Club" that everyone was beginning to know by heart.

TikTok users started splicing the old video with new ones of her on the Midwest Princess or Guts Tours. Although she sang the song almost exactly the same, the juxtaposition was dramatic: Not only was her look a major glow-up, but in the recent clips her massive audience screamed the words while she danced. Just two years prior she had seemed almost ordinary singing alone, barely moving behind her keyboard. The re-spliced clips went viral.

PREVIOUS
Chappell at the Grammy Museum in Los Angeles on November 7, 2024.

Of course, Chappell had been on social media since the beginning, and on TikTok since 2020. She told *Rolling Stone*, "I wasn't sleeping . . . I was on the incorrect meds. I had the energy and the delusion and realized that this app is fueled off of mental illness. Straight up." The magazine *The Face* called it "relatable agent-of-chaos energy," and fans loved the authenticity.

But truthfully, Chappell found it frustrating. She told *Cherwell*, "I can't really hate on it because it's pushed me forward and people know about me because of it, though it's the most soul-sucking part of my job . . . It's not hard. It's a fifteen-second video. But that's not the point. To some people, it comes naturally, and those people really soar, so it makes you feel bad about yourself if you try hard and it doesn't work. To be honest, any video that I put out about my music automatically doesn't do as well as a video of me doing something stupid, saying something nonsensical."

In Chappell's case, she didn't go viral on TikTok and then became a star. She became a star and then went viral. *The Washington Post* wrote, "The algorithms love her. But she resonates with humans, too. Roan is the kind of queer pop star who seems ready-made for the moment: referential, silly in a messy way yet aesthetically precise, and one of a kind." *Billboard* agreed. A month after her *Tiny Desk* appearance, they wrote, "She didn't pander to TikTok or get lucky on Spotify algorithms (though TikTok obviously played a role), she just had a label that knew how to use her and

> "I can't really hate on it because it's pushed me forward and people know about me because of it, though it's the most soul-sucking part of my job."

a live show that sparked genuine word-of-mouth. The hardest part of the music industry at all levels is getting people to care about your music, and Roan has given audiences reasons to care—whether it's the music, the over-the-top aesthetic, or the inspiring backstory of a woman from Missouri coming to terms with her identity."

In April 2024, Chappell did something wholly unpredictable and released another single. Called "Good Luck, Babe!", it was written back in 2022 with Dan and Justin, around the time that the three of them had written "My Kink is Karma." They had left it unfinished because, Dan explained to *Hits Daily Double*, "Chappell and I couldn't crack the code on the song." But just before the holidays, one day at Dan's studio, she asked him to open it back up. At that point, it was just called "Good Luck!" Chappell wrote some more. She wanted it to include a name—maybe "Good Luck, Jane?" Dan started playing around with the synthesized string sound that would open the song. "In January, we said, 'This is the next song we're going to release,'" he recalled. "And then we wrote the bridge—well, she wrote most of the bridge; that's her."

"It was definitely one of the hardest songs to get right," Dan agreed to *Billboard*. About the song, the magazine said she was "in rare form" and that "Good Luck, Babe!" showed "a previously unseen depth to her sound." Dan knew it was a great song, but he wasn't thinking too much about the reception when they released it. "Did I think it was going to be a hit? I did not," he told *Hits Daily Double*. "I will admit that I did not know. I don't think anybody felt like this was the song that was going to change everything." It would become her first song to hit one billion streams on Spotify.

The Festival Queen

Chappell wasn't going viral just for her *Tiny Desk* concert and new single. During the second and third weekends of April, she had performed two concerts at Coachella that also seemed to turn the tide. Later, *Harper's Bazaar* would interview Misha, who was gaining notoriety of her own as Chappell's creative director, and ask her if there was a moment she and Chappell both felt that something had shifted, in terms of fame. "Coachella" was her answer. "That festival was such a turning point because of how big the crowd was," she said. It was a moment they would probably never forget.

Not only had Chappell never played a festival, she had never even been to one before. As early as 2018, she had been telling interviewers that she wanted to play at a summer music festival, but only the top-drawing artists got a slot. In order to carve the way forward, Kiely and another of Chappell's agents, Jackie Nalpant, had personally taken festival bookers to some of her shows, so they could see her stage presence firsthand. "Coachella was a paradigm shift," Jackie later told the *Times*.

"I'm your favorite artist's favorite artist," she declared.

Beforehand, Chappell and Misha enjoyed the festival, waiting in line for the Ferris Wheel like any other normal Coachella attendee. Misha would later recall it being one of the last times they could be "normal" in a public setting like that. Her set the first weekend, Chappell wore a white latex shirt emblazoned with the words "Eat Me" along with a studded collar, and debuted "Good Luck, Babe!" in front of '90s-esque, 8-bit animations that Misha had stayed up all night making. The new song was shared—and shared again—across social media.

"The first weekend was crowded. The second weekend, you couldn't get near the tent," Jackie! later recalled to *Hits Daily Double*. The second time around, Chappell emerged as a giant pink butterfly. "I'm your favorite artist's favorite artist," she declared, in a nod to drag queen Sasha Colby, and the crowd went wild.

She seemed a little tentative at first, but soon, she had pulled off the top portion of her wings and took full control of the crowd. Chappell "delivered the kind of goose-bump-giving, star-making, history-in-real-time performance that doesn't often happen these days. And her life hasn't been the same since," *Rolling Stone* wrote. Her streaming numbers had more than doubled from March, now as high as 36.6 million weekly streams.

Lesbian Pop and Brat Summer

When the queer artist Charli XCX released her album *Brat* on June 7, 2024, she had no idea she was kicking off what would come to be known as "Brat Summer." Of course, brats have been around forever, and perhaps reached peak popularity in the '80s, when a group of hot young actors were dubbed "the Brat Pack" (a pun on "the Rat Pack" of the '60s). But as Charli explained it, a brat was "that girl who is a little messy and likes to party and maybe says some dumb things sometimes. Who feels herself but maybe also has a breakdown. But kind [of] parties through it, is very honest, very blunt. A little bit volatile. Like, does dumb things. But it's brat. You're brat. That's brat."

Soon, the label was being applied to a bevy of young female artists who had success that summer, including Chappell, Olivia, Reneé Rapp, Taylor Swift, Billie Eilish, and Sabrina Carpenter. The queer contingent (Charli, Chappell, Reneé, and Billie) was striking. "Gone are the days of love sick ponderings about a boy," wrote gay publication *EDGE*. "But lesbian 'brat' pop isn't just about ditching boys and having fun; it's about defiance . . . [so] perhaps it makes sense that Chappell Roan is the undeniable leader of the pack."

#Bratsummer started on TikTok, but no one loved it more than media outlets and others needing a hook. The phrase soon dominated headlines, memes, and even political campaigns. Morning talk show hosts explained the term to their viewers, and the *Collins Dictionary* named "brat" its 2024 Word of the Year. It described a brat as someone having "a confident, independent, and hedonistic attitude."

In May, Chappell played Alabama's Hangout Fest and at Boston Calling, where she performed to 40,000 people—more than some headliners—during the 4 p.m. time slot. "I would wager that a lot of people probably bought tickets to see Megan [Thee Stallion] and Hozier and The Killers, and then in the subsequent months found themselves becoming big fans of Chappell Roan," the festival's booking director told *The Washington Post*.

Chappell's streaming numbers continued to skyrocket as she took over festival after festival. In June, for New York's Governors Ball, she and her stylist Genesis concocted her most iconic costume to date: Chappell as the Statue of Liberty, complete with a shimmering skirt and shiny crown. Her entire body was painted pale green, even her butt cheeks—you could tell because, as was often the case that summer, they were completely exposed. Rolled onto stage in a partially eaten red apple, she broke out in front of the massive audience before opening the show with "Femininomenon." Misha would tell *Harper's Bazaar* that it was another breakthrough moment: "That's when we knew, 'Okay, we're officially on everyone's mood board.'"

By now, Chappell had perfected her show, playing a perfect set that not only got the fans who were near the stage hopping up and down, but the audience members at the back of the crowd involved too. She paced the stage like a seasoned rock star, pointing, gesturing, and

"That's when we knew, 'Okay, we're officially on everyone's mood board.'" Misha told **Harper's Bazaar.**

inviting the audience to sing along. The way Chappell sang songs live also emphasized her vocal talents, mixing in some slower songs and belting out lines in a strong and steady voice that many pop stars simply couldn't muster.

Chappell was also great at talking to the audience, and smart enough to know that a simple, "Where my girls at?" could go a long way. The way she introduced songs—"Are you ready to get 'Naked in Manhattan'?"—not only got fans excited, but reinforced the name of the song, just in case they wanted to stream it later. Everything was geared toward inclusivity, maximum fun, and even euphoria at getting to be part of the moment. "Can you believe it? We're at —!" she'd yell, filling in the name of the festival.

At Governors Ball, Chappell changed her script and instead used her platform to speak about human rights. "I am in drag as the biggest queen of all," she told the crowd, "but in case you had forgotten what's etched on my pretty little toes, 'Give me your tired, your poor; your huddled masses yearning to breathe free.' That means freedom in trans rights, that means freedom in women's rights, and it especially means freedom for all oppressed people in occupied territories," she said, tearing up.

She also changed her typical call-out before "My Kink Is Karma." Normally, she'd shout-out an ex, saying, "I dedicate this song to my ex," adding, "How does it feel to become everything you hated, and I became everything I wanted?!" But at Governors Ball, she looked right into the camera and said, "I dedicate this song as a response to the White House, who asked me to perform for Pride. We want liberty, freedom, and justice for all. When you do that, that's when I'll come!" An incredibly gutsy

"I dedicate this song as a response to the White House, who asked me to perform for Pride. We want liberty, freedom, and justice for all. When you do that, that's when I'll come!"

thing to say during an election year (when liberals are often criticized for speaking out against other liberals), the revelation made a lot more headlines than her usual shout-out to her ex.

Later, she told Bowen Yang of *Interview* magazine how difficult speaking up at Governors Ball was for her. "It was hard to be like, 'I'm going to say something that a lot of my family is going to be like, Wow, you crossed the line.' It's emotional because I believe what I said, and what's sad is that me believing in who I am, and what I stand for, rubs against a lot of my home."

Fortunately, any acceptance she wasn't getting from her hometown, her audience was sure to fill in the gaps and more. A Chappell fan who attended her show in Columbus, Ohio, and wrote about it for WSOE, the local radio station, said, "Celebration truly was the best word for the energy in the crowd. I talked to those around me about what seeing Chappell live meant to them, and what I heard solidified her as a queer idol. Many spoke about how her music made them feel seen as a queer person, even if they weren't out, and how the success of Chappell, who herself is a lesbian, meant a great deal for representation in popular culture."

PREVIOUS
Chappell performing at Governors Ball in New York City on June 9, 2024.

OPPOSITE
Chappell performs at Outside Lands at Golden Gate Park in San Francisco on August 11, 2024.

> *"Where you are, exactly who you are right now, you don't need to be anything more, and you are loved and cherished for who you are. I love you and I cherish you and that's coming from a gay [girl] from the Midwest."*

In 2024, in Iowa, she played the Hinterland Fest. And at the Westfair Amphitheater in Council Bluffs, she told 15,000 people (her largest audience yet for a headlining show), "Where you are, exactly who you are right now, you don't need to be anything more, and you are loved and cherished for who you are. I love you and I cherish you and that's coming from a gay [girl] from the Midwest."

After Governors Ball, the pivotal moments seemed to keep coming as images of her dressed as Lady Liberty kept proliferating online. A week later, Chappell performed to a giant crowd at Bonnaroo in Tennessee, where concert organizers had upgraded her to the main stage. At the end of June, she appeared on *The Tonight Show Starring Jimmy Fallon*, performing "Good Luck, Babe!" and sitting down for an interview with the host. Genesis created a special look for the appearance, which incorporated a dress adorned with giant black feathers; a frizzy, blonde wig; and super-long, white fingernails that she gently tapped together to applaud herself as Jimmy read a list of her recent accomplishments. "I just wanted to make something that I could party to and other people could party to and something that I would never be sad or bored performing," she told Jimmy, who said he was a fan.

Chappell performs at GLAAD's #SpiritDay concert in Los Angeles, California, on October 19, 2022.

TRACK 5

CHAPPELL THE STAR

"By the time Roan took the stage in Chicago's Grant Park on August 1, Lollapalooza had become Chappellpalooza," *Rolling Stone* wrote in its cover story on Chappell. "Based on both the bootleg merch stalls around the Loop and the overhead drone footage of the audience, Roan has become the de facto owner of the pink cowboy hat, whose previous keepers were Harry Styles and Barbie."

Chappell played to what was estimated to be the largest crowd in Lollapalooza history: 80,000 people, plus more than a dozen HD cameras capturing it all to stream live on Hulu. The drone footage was truly astonishing to anyone who had ever been to Chicago—the entirety of Millennium and Grant Park along the lake filled with humans of all kinds singing, screaming, and later in the show, doing the "HOT TO GO!" dance.

When she took the stage, it seemed that just about everyone had their phone out to capture the moment. Over ethereal music, her band came out alongside muscular bodybuilders in front of a pink screen that said, "Chappell Wrestling." A voice-over announced, "You only get to call me one thing: I am the Midwest Princess!" Chappell came out wearing a pink-and-blue costume reminiscent of a Mexican Lucha Libre wrestler, including the full-face mask. Before she removed it, she shed a few tears in awe. As she started to sing "Femininomenon," you could hear the audience singing along. When she said, "Can you believe it? We're at Lollapalooza!" the responding roar was deafening. She introduced herself to the audience twice during her set, not seeming to realize they were all there for her.

PREVIOUS
Chappell performs a high-energy yet heartfelt show at Lollapalooza in Chicago's Grant Park on August 1, 2024.

> *"It's Chappell's world and we're just living in it," Lollapalooza wrote on its own social media.*

Chappell gave a masterful performance in Chicago, singing twelve songs, including all of her pop hits and a couple of ballads. "It's Chappell's world and we're just living in it," Lollapalooza wrote on its own social media. Coming from a long way since the beginning, Chappell was not only comfortable, she was flirty. "This song goes out to the girl in the mini skirt and go-go boots," she told the crowd before singing "Red Wine Supernova." "I know she's here. I saw her in the crowd. She's got canine teeth like a vampire. If you see her, tell her she's my red wine supernova!"

The stage they had upgraded her to was simply massive, and the bodybuilders did their best to take up the room that would normally be filled with dancers, giant backing bands, and elaborate stage props of a more established artist. For the finish, Devon walked down the catwalk into the audience, while Chappell sang to her on her knees. By the time she closed with "Pink Pony Club" it was obvious to everyone–the audience, the music industry, the entire world–that Chappell Roan was a superstar.

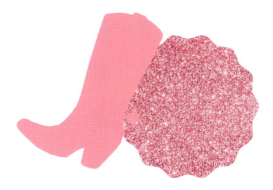

Chappell's Influences

Drag Is Here to Stay

Drag has been lurking at the fringes of American entertainment since at least 1867, the year of the first recorded drag ball in Harlem. It continued to be part of US history: In the 1900s, several "female impersonators" found success in vaudeville. In the 1930s, drag queens known as "pansies" were hits at nightclubs in New York and Miami. Then in 1972, John Waters made history by giving his favorite drag queen, Divine, a starring role in his film *Pink Flamingos*. (Her look would go on to inspire Ursula, the octopus queen from Disney's *The Little Mermaid*.)

"Drag is like a spa for my soul," Chappell told *The Guardian*. She's cited drag as an inspiration since before she started considering herself a drag queen ("Yes, Chappell Roan is a drag queen—and yes, women can do drag," *Out* magazine clarified). She's praised drag queens' beauty, confidence, silliness, camp sensibility, and ability to bring joy to audiences. She also loves their aesthetic. "I think Chappell's a drag-queen version of me because it's very larger-than-life, kind of tacky, not afraid to say really lewd things," she told *Vanity Fair*.

The most famous drag queen of all time is undoubtedly RuPaul, who began performing in the 1980s and started hosting her influential TV show *RuPaul's Drag Race* in 2009. Chappell's favorite drag queens—including Sasha Colby, Trixie Mattel, Katya Zamolodchikova, Crystal Methyd, and Mo Heart—have all appeared on the series.

Tequila Thirst supporting Chappell Roan during the Midwest Princess Tour in Manchester, UK on September 13, 2024.

"You only get to call me one thing: I am the Midwest Princess!"

The Freakiness of Fame

Chappell's success certainly wasn't overnight, but it was sudden. "It's been pretty incredible, to say the least," Dan told *The Washington Post* in his role as head of her label. "I always felt deep down in my heart that we were creating something really special and that it was just going to take a minute for the world to catch on to it. And so, to see it start to happen, it just feels insane . . . It's kind of what I was always dreaming for her."

During the week leading up to Fourth of July weekend, Chappell garnered more than eighty-two million song streams in the US, the *Post* reported. The paper determined it was more than a 1,600 percent increase since *The Rise and Fall of a Midwest Princess* released. By August, the album had belatedly hit the *Billboard* Top 10. She appeared on the cover of *Rolling Stone* with the headline "A Star is Born," and a few months later was on the cover of *NME*, which wrote, "Pop connoisseurs are queuing up to worship at the altar of Chappell Roan."

New fans went down self-induced rabbit holes, obsessively consuming singles—that had taken her years to release—in rapid succession. Was this year's "Good Luck, Babe!" the best Chappell Roan song, or was it

PREVIOUS
Chappell attending the 67th Annual Grammy Awards on February 2, 2025.

"I always felt deep down in my heart that we were creating something really special and that it was just going to take a minute for the world to catch on to it," Dan told **The Washington Post**.

last year's "Femininomenon" or "HOT TO GO!"? What about 2020's "Pink Pony Club"? After going months, even years, without making the charts, suddenly her songs all charted at the same time—by September, there were six Chappell Roan songs in the *Billboard* US Hot 100, and three were in the UK Top 40. Ever since Governors Ball, "I was getting almost a hundred thousand followers a day," she told *Rolling Stone*. "At first, I was in severe denial . . . They would literally show me some stats and the only thing I could do is say, 'No, no, no. It's not like that.'" She was completely overwhelmed—she had more than two hundred unanswered texts on her phone.

"Roan has experienced the kind of rise that makes words like 'meteoric' feel quaint," Brittany Spanos wrote in *Rolling Stone*. Chappell had always experienced exhaustion and anxiety around too much interaction with the public, but now the attention from fans started to feel even more intense. "Idolizing someone is so weird!" she told *Vulture*. "People think they know me as a person when Chappell Roan is literally a performance piece. Chappell is a character. I'm Kayleigh, and I am scared of people who have made a version of me in their heads that they think is theirs," she explained. She was always touched when fans told her how much her music meant to them, but "I'm very turned off by the celebrity of it all," she told *The Guardian*.

She loved her fans, but interacting with them could be a lot to deal with. Fans came up to her while she was watching drag shows and asked for selfies. One person requested a picture while she was actively having a fight with her girlfriend. And at a bar one night, someone walked right up to her and kissed her—what many would consider to be sexual assault. She told *The Face* about an experience in Syracuse that seemed to say it all: "I was crying on the phone to my therapist. I was like, 'I don't know what's going on. This is scary. People are coming up to me, and I don't want to talk to them most of the time, because I'm freaked out.' I'm like, literally crying on the phone outside, on the sidewalk, and this [girl] comes up to me, and she's like, 'Hey, I'm sorry. I'm so sorry to bother you, but are you Chappell Roan?'" Soon, Chappell even had to change therapists because her current one wasn't experienced enough with clients dealing with fame.

What would her breaking point be? "I'm going to quit if I ever have a bodyguard," she told *Paper* in June. But by September, she had to take a security guard to the thrift store. "My whole life has changed," she told Kate Solomon at *The Guardian*. "Everything that I really love to do now comes with baggage . . . I have to book security and prepare myself that this is not going to be normal. Going to the park, Pilates, yoga—how do I do this in a safe way where I'm not going to be stalked or harassed?" Kate pointed out a hard truth: "She spent years building a community where queer people like her can feel safe and now fame has robbed her of that feeling."

"My whole life has changed. Everything that I really love to do now comes with baggage."

Online, people not only gushed about her songs, debated their favorite Chappell looks, and shared stories about attending her shows—they criticized her every move. "You are never enough as an artist," she told *Vulture*. "I release a song, and I go live on TikTok that day, like, 'Hey guys, "Red Wine Supernova" is out!' Do you know what a lot of the comments are? 'When's the next one coming out?' The expectation is insane." One commenter complained that she needed to stop shaving her armpits. Some worried she didn't use the word "lesbian" enough. Others revealed that her uncle was a Republican who held a state office—did that mean she was secretly a Republican too? A debate broke out on the Chappell Roan subreddit about the Kidz Bop version of "Good Luck, Babe!" asking if Chappell had given her OK on the new lyrics, which erased all mentions of queerness?

But perhaps nothing stirred as much controversy as her refusal to make an endorsement in the 2024 presidential election between Donald Trump and Kamala Harris. Finally, Chappell had had enough. She posted a video bluntly saying, "If you look at my statement and you're still like, she's just playing both sides . . . No. You're not getting it . . . I'm critiquing both sides because they're both so [messed] up . . . I can't put my name and my entire project behind one."

"People think they know me as a person when Chappell Roan is literally a performance piece. Chappell is a character. I'm Kayleigh."

After someone got her dad's phone number and called him, she also took to TikTok to directly address creepy fan behavior, saying, "Just answer my questions for a second: If you saw a random woman on the street, would you yell at her from the car window? Would you harass her in public? Would you go up to a random lady and say, 'Can I get a photo with you?' and she's like, 'No. What the [heck]?' and then you get mad at this random lady? Would you be offended if she says no to your time because she has her own time? Would you stalk her family? Would you follow her around? Would you try to dissect her life and bully her online? This is a lady you don't know, and she doesn't know you at all. Would you assume that she's a good person; assume she's a bad person; would you assume everything you read about her online is true? I'm a random [person]. You're a random [person]. Just think about that for a second, OK?"

Going about it the only way she knew how, Chappell struggled to put her fans in their place, but she may have been making the situation even worse. In the videos, with no makeup, in a basic gray tee, even admitting in one to having just woken up, she might have had better luck if Genesis had made her into her traditional Chappell look, then told everyone to leave Kayleigh alone. Instead, she was creating an intimate space for her audience to get to know Kayleigh, while telling them they had no idea who she was.

PREVIOUS
Chappell attending Universal Music Group's 2024 After Party in Los Angeles, California, in the costume she wore for the cover image of her song "Good Luck, Babe!" on February 4, 2024.

OPPOSITE
In the midst of her Midwest Princess Tour, Chappell played the Kentucky Pride Festival on June 15, 2024.

The difference between Chappell and Kayleigh was more than just her makeup and clothes. Even though she was dating women now, the gap between herself and the character she created to live out her wildest dreams was still gaping wide. Her song "Casual" was a great example. Based on the long-distance relationship she had during the pandemic, which fizzled out shortly after meeting in real life, the lyrics elaborated on the theme of feeling betrayed with numerous scenarios that never happened. "I was really nervous because it's pretty crass," Chappell admitted to Sam Prance. But it would become one of her best-known songs, even if it was fictional.

So, while Kayleigh admitted to the Associated Press that the person who originally inspired the song "totally had the right to say it's casual" (they never even progressed past kissing, after all!), in the song, Chappell is sad and enraged. "I had to redo this song several times because I was not being sad enough. I was not being relatable enough. I've never recorded a song like that. To get in that headspace was really hurtful," she told *Rolling Stone*.

> "My songs are so overtly sexual on purpose because it's an expression of me that I wasn't able to express growing up in a Christian household, in a Christian town that was very conservative."

Meanwhile, her mother hated it. "My mom can't stand 'Casual,'" she admitted to *Pop Crave*. "She's like, '[that's] so gross! Why'd you have to say that?!' I was like, 'Just be crazy! I don't know. Say something bold!'" To *Vulture*, she explained, "My songs are so overtly sexual on purpose because it's an expression of me that I wasn't able to express growing up in a Christian household, in a Christian town that was very conservative."

After all the harassment and constant expectation for more, more, more, it turned out that having a separate persona in Chappell was becoming the key to coping with her fame. "It's too much to process if I don't have division between the two," she told *Vulture*. "It hurts my feelings when people say mean things about me online. But it doesn't hurt my feelings as much if they're saying it about Chappell. Then it's just them commenting on the art. I have to remind myself all the time: Art is meant to be judged. That's the whole point. It does hurt less if I'm just like, 'Okay, they're judging the project. They don't know who I am. They're not saying I'm a bad person.'"

With things getting even crazier, the separation also allowed her to take a break. "I just can't be here all the time. It's just too much," she told the *Hollywood Reporter*. When she wasn't performing, she wore drab colors like white, black, and gray. "I felt like I needed to go the complete opposite so I could calm down," she told *Vanity Fair*. "Same with my room. My room has calming colors, and I have a storage unit where I keep all my boas and everything, so I don't have to look at it 'cause it's so much."

But even as Kayleigh worked to separate Chappell from herself, popularity—and its breakneck schedule—was bearing down on her. It was becoming too much not only to wrap her head around this person called Chappell, but also Chappell's sudden and extreme celebrity. "This type of year does something to people," she told the *Hollywood Reporter*. "Every big thing that happens in someone's career happened in five months for me . . . It's so crazy that things I never thought would happen, happened times ten. I think that just really rocked my system. I don't know what a good mental health routine looks like for me right now."

As *Vulture* put it, "It would be impossible for anyone's sense of themselves to expand at the exponential rate Roan's public profile has . . . [She] hasn't had the time to learn how to protect herself against the glare of the spotlight, nor to gain the financial resources other celebrities use to cosset themselves from the world. She's fallen into an unmanageable level of notoriety: famous enough to have stalkers, not rich enough to hole up on Lake Como."

"Every big thing that happens in someone's career happened in five months for me... It's so crazy that things I never thought would happen, happened times ten."

When Elton Calls

There were some upsides to stardom. Of course, there was the fact that she could now pay her rent without worry, something that was still relatively new for her. She could get free tickets to any show she could ever dream of and could bring as many friends as she wanted. She was able to give back—she set up a trust to give out free tickets to people who couldn't afford her concerts, gave portions of her proceeds to LGBTQ+ nonprofits, and sold items at merch stands that went to aid for Palestine.

She had the ability to create more and more amazing shows, hiring even more artists to help her build her world. "She lights up as she talks about how bigger budgets and more agency have transformed her shows," Kate Solomon wrote in *The Guardian*. She especially loved having a makeup artist. "I love it," she told *Paper*. "I don't have to carry anything. Everything is new and different. Every week, I'm just like, 'Makeup artist please help me! I need your help!'"

Perhaps the weirdest thing about becoming famous, however, was receiving a call from Elton John. An unknown number kept trying to audio message her on iCloud and just kept calling and calling. "I thought a [crazy] fan found my iCloud," she related to *Rolling Stone*. "I was so mad and was about to hand my phone to my friend like, 'Yo, let's prank them.' . . . I finally answered it one day, and it was Elton [freak]ing John." He was a fan and reached out after seeing her social media posts about

Your Favorite Artist's Favorite Artist

"I'm your favorite artist's favorite artist," Chappell famously proclaimed at Coachella 2024. Here are some of the artists who admire her.

Olivia Rodrigo. One of Chappell's biggest supporters, Olivia told her audience, "I think [Chappell] is one of the most singular, inspiring, powerful artists," before introducing her for a duet of "HOT TO GO!"

Adele. After hearing a Chappell Roan song at her birthday party, Adele told concert-goers that she "went down a rabbit hole" listening to her "brilliant songs."

Beyoncé. Beyoncé told *GQ* she thought Chappell was "talented and interesting," which *People* called "as good as being anointed official pop royalty."

Elton John. After discovering Chappell via "Pink Pony Club," Elton told her on his podcast, "You make my heart jump when I see you, when I hear you."

Sabrina Carpenter. Sabrina admitted to *Rolling Stone* that "I've been just as obsessed with her as everyone has" and sang a cover of "Good Luck, Babe!" on BBC's *Radio 1 Live Lounge*.

SZA. SZA was so inspired by Chappell's epic 2024 Lollapalooza performance that she posted, "She makes me wanna keep making music n art forever."

the public's sometimes-disturbing behavior. He invited her over for pizza with his husband, and she took Dan with her. "I am very protective of her," Elton told *Rolling Stone*. "She is kind, innocent, and wonderful. She is not 'Chappell Roan' offstage—a bit like me."

When she wasn't sharing Elton John's pizza with Dan, she shared her success with her family. "It's fun that my parents are so supportive. It's just cool to see my family get excited about things that we never thought were possible," she told *The Guardian*. Although it could be tough for them, living in a small town and having a daughter as outspoken—and now, as famous—as Chappell, "they don't put other people's concerns over my happiness," she told Adam Lisicky on his podcast. She often shouted-out her mom onstage. For the Fourth of July that year, she even went back home to spend time with her family. "You would have loved the shows, the songs, the music videos, and the feeling of the crowd singing with me," she wrote in a letter to her late grandfather on Instagram.

Still, her mental health suffered. In a candid moment after pulling out of a couple of festivals, she told Kate Solomon, "Every time I walk through my front door, it just comes out of me . . . I can't even help it, I just start sobbing [at] either being so angry at myself for choosing this path or grieving how the curiosity and pure wonder I had about the world is somewhat taken away from me." Her new therapist diagnosed her with extreme depression. As usual, she was determined to fight. "I feel ambitious about making this sustainable," she resolutely told *The Face*. "That's my biggest goal right now. My brain is like: quit right

"It's just cool to see my family get excited about things that we never thought were possible."

now, take next year off . . . This industry and artistry [fricking] thrive on mental illness, burnout, overworking yourself, overextending yourself, not sleeping . . . The ambition is: how do I not hate myself, my job, my life, and do this?" Some of the ways she found to protect herself were reminding herself that unreasonable expectations were not her fault and encouraging herself to say "no."

Chappell was back to where she was as a child, feeling frustrated, stuck, and constrained by what other people wanted for her. But this time, there was one big difference. She had friends to reach out to for support. In addition to having Misha by her side throughout it all, she also found that the currently reigning pop princesses were also real people, and they were there for her. When a man started yelling at her at the airport for not wanting to autograph the Chappell Roan merchandise he was hoping to sell on the internet, Lorde sent her a list of eight things she wished she had known about air travel as a celebrity. "Hey, I feel crazy. I know you feel crazy," Sabrina Carpenter texted her. Mitski, Billie Eilish, Charli XCX, Reneé Rapp, Phoebe Bridgers, Lizzo, Katy Perry, and Lady Gaga have also reached out, especially after Chappell spoke out about her mental health.

"The pop girls that you and I have loved our whole lives . . . a lot of them have reached out and are so supportive," Chappell said on TikTok. "It's so sick to know that the girls . . . [are] really supporting each other in the pop industry . . . It makes me believe in the world."

FOLLOWING
Sabrina Carpenter, Chappell Roan, and Billie Eilish attending the 67th Annual Grammy Awards on February 2, 2025.

"It's so sick to know that the girls ... [are] really supporting each other in the pop industry ... It makes me believe in the world."

The Top of Pop Mountain

After her electrifying, Joan of Arc–inspired performance at the Video Music Awards that saw her realizing her dream of shooting a flaming arrow into a set piece, something even better happened: Chappell won Best New Artist. Wearing sparkly chainmail complete with a matching hood, opera gloves, and silver fingernails, she took the stage again and yelled, "Can you believe it? We're at the VMAs!" But for the first time all year, it didn't sound like she actually believed it.

"Uh, I wrote a speech in my diary," she told the crowd, before reading somewhat timidly from a black book. "Thank you, MTV, and Island Records, and my team, and my family and friends," she said with a giggle. Then, to wild cheers: "I dedicate this to all the drag artists who inspire me." She wagged her finger at the crowd and her voice gained steam. "And I dedicate this to queer and trans–fueled pop all around. To the gays who dedicate my songs to someone they love–or hate. And thank you to the people who are fans who listen to me, who hear me when I share my joy and my fears. Thank you for listening to me." The crowd screamed in appreciation, and Chappell laughed. "And for all the queer kids in the Midwest watching right now: I see you, I understand you, because I'm one of you," she continued. Her voice turned theatrical. "And don't let anyone ever tell you that you can't be exactly who you wanna be."

> *"And thank you to the people who are fans who listen to me, who hear me when I share my joy and my fears. Thank you for listening to me."*

If the "femininomenonal ascent of Chappell to the summit of Pop Mountain" (as *The Face* called it) had been hard for Chappell to comprehend so far, the most mind-blowing part of her climb came in October when she appeared on *Saturday Night Live*. Naturally, she took her whole crew with her—Misha, Genesis, even Ryan came and took photos backstage—and she hired set designer Maris Jones to make special pieces for her songs. *Harper's Bazaar* sent a reporter to see her get ready for the show and talk to Misha. "It's like when you're at a competition and you're out of state and you're in a hotel room all together—that's what the vibe is," Misha told them. "This is kind of the grand finale of the year—it's like, 'We made it to nationals!' We keep making jokes about this, being like, 'We're on a cheer team'—like the night before the VMAs, we were like, 'If we get this, we're going to regionals!' It's silly, but it's what it feels like. After this, we're back to LA, and it feels like the perfect way to end the year."

On a more serious note, she told them that Chappell performing on *SNL* felt completely different than her festival shows. "*SNL* reaches a totally different audience," she explained. "Your parents could be watching! When it's TV, people at home are just tuning in . . . It's almost like a talent show—what is the audience going to remember if this is their first time seeing the artist?" For the episode promos, Chappell wore another stunning costume, commissioning a custom-crafted look by designer

Gunnar Deatherage inspired by 1900s showgirls. It featured hand-sewn details and vintage circus charms and took more than five hundred man-hours to complete.

Because it was so delicate, she performed in more traditional dresses and let Maris's sets stand out. She sang "Pink Pony Club," then took a risk by debuting a new song, "The Giver." Not only was it untested, it was a country song–and unabashedly lesbian. Yet she pulled it off, and not just because of her perky gingham outfit. She introduced herself to an even bigger audience, and got her current audience excited for a new single.

Less than a week later, the Grammy nominations were announced. Sadly, Chappell and Misha didn't get a nod for package design, but she got six other nominations, including Album of the Year for *The Rise and Fall of a Midwest Princess.* At the February 2025 ceremony, she won Best New Artist.

It was a show befitting a princess, including Chappell's numerous outfit changes. On the red carpet, she donned a gown by Jean Paul Gaultier that featured Degas-inspired ballerinas. Then she changed into a blue corseted dress before she was seated. For her performance of "Pink Pony Club," she became a rhinestone-clad cowgirl (again, in a corset). And for her final look, she wore a unique, scrunched-up wraparound dress with a party hat so huge it looked like a hat a wizard would wear. Her table was front and center; on her right was Misha, and on her left was Dan, who would end up winning Producer of the Year.

When Chappell took the stage to accept her award for Best New Artist, as usual, she took her moment to speak out. "I told myself if I ever won a Grammy, and I got to stand up here in front of the most powerful people in music," she said, "I would demand that labels and the industry, profiting millions of dollars off of artists, would offer a livable wage in healthcare, especially to developing artists." She told the story of getting dropped, and having no support, and challenged the recording conglomerates to do better. "Labels, we got you, but do you got us?" she asked. Dan wiped away tears; her fellow artists cheered. The next day, she made headlines. There's no doubt the music industry took notice.

The rest of the year would see Chappell continuing to take over the universe—or at least, her corner of it. She donated to a fund to help developing artists afford healthcare, officially released "The Giver," and even became a guest judge on *RuPaul's Drag Race All-Stars*.

FOLLOWING
Chappell performs her debut album, *The Rise and Fall of a Midwest Princess* at the House of Blues in Chicago, Illinois, on October 5, 2023.

"Don't let anyone ever tell you that you can't be exactly who you wanna be."

EPILOGUE

THE NEXT TRACKLIST

Chappell caused a major shift in the music industry beyond just her success as an independent artist and her Grammy speech. She was officially a gay icon. "I don't know if anyone that does this and is involved in queer music intends to be part of a revolution," Chappell's drummer, Lucy, who is also queer, told Iowa Public Radio. "I think you are who you are, and suddenly people have interest in that, and that's when change happens. It's not by performative actions. It's not by trying to be something you're not so you get fame. I think Chappell, she works really hard. She's been herself, and people are interested in that." By breaking free of the shackles of a giant record label and creating something that was true to herself, Chappell gave girls and women of all ages new courage to be their authentic selves, especially if that involved having feelings for other women.

For now, thanks to the backing of her fan base and having found the right partnerships, Chappell is able to keep that authenticity close. "I can only do what I'm best at, which is writing and singing music. That makes me feel free and happens to make a lot of other people feel free," she told a Brown University student reporter in 2023. "I'm just going to try to write songs that I absolutely love, but I don't have a plan," she told Elton John on his podcast. Dan is also in no rush. "Kayleigh and I are not the people who go in the studio and write a song in one day. We take our time with it," he told *Billboard*.

> *"I can only do what I'm best at, which is writing and singing music. That makes me feel free and happens to make a lot of other people feel free."*

"We've been putting together some silly ideas," Misha told *Harper's Bazaar*, "and it's fun to know because we did it all from scratch the first time. We know now that we have the resources to do more, but also there's power in knowing we could also strip it all back. We can do anything, and it feels like the world is our mood board." As long as Chappell keeps her authenticity, there is no doubt she will continue to produce art that audiences connect with. If anyone can do it in the monolithic music business, Chappell can.

In addition to resisting political endorsements, she's also resisted brand deals. "My career has worked because I've done it my way, and I've not compromised morals and time," she told Bowen Yang for *Interview* magazine. "I have not succumbed to the pressure. Like, '[Girl], I'm not doing a brand deal if it doesn't feel right. I don't care how much you're paying me.' That's why I can sleep at night." She has said she doesn't feel an obligation to be morally perfect and is trying to take her status as a queer icon in stride, without feeling like a spokesperson for the entire community.

But the biggest key to her authenticity is letting her inner child guide her work. "When I realized that I should dedicate my career to honoring the childhood I never got, it got big quick," she told *The Face*. As she told her fans on TikTok, "I don't care about anything else, except giving space to people to be free. Because that's what I needed so bad: freedom."

PREVIOUS
Chappell has a heart-to-heart with fans onstage at New York's Governors Ball on June 9, 2024.

FOLLOWING
Chappell performing at Elton John AIDS Foundation's 33rd Annual Academy Awards Viewing Party in West Hollywood, California, on March 2, 2025.

"My career has worked because I've done it my way, and I've not compromised morals and time. I have not succumbed to the pressure."

Discography

School Nights EP

Original Release Date: September 22, 2017
Record Label: Atlantic Records
Singles:
- "Good Hurt" (August 3, 2017)
- "Die Young" (September 22, 2017)

Sales: Unknown

Other singles unaffiliated with an album:
- "Bitter" (February 1, 2018)
- "School Nights" (March 16, 2018)
- "Love Me Anyway" (May 1, 2020)
- "Good Luck, Babe!" (April 5, 2024)
- "The Subway" (unreleased)
- "The Giver" (March 14, 2025)

The Rise and Fall of a Midwest Princess

Original Release Date: September 22, 2023
Record Label: Island Records
Singles:
- "Pink Pony Club" (August 3, 2020)
- "California" (May 29, 2020)
- "Naked In Manhattan" (February 18, 2022)
- "My Kink Is Karma" (May 6, 2022)
- "Femininomenon" (August 12, 2022)
- "Casual" (October 28, 2022)
- "Kaleidoscope" (March 31, 2023)
- "Red Wine Supernova" (May 17, 2023)
- "HOT TO GO!" (August 11, 2023)

Sales: 1 million copies (US)

Chappell gets ready before a performance at the House of Blues in Chicago in October 2023.

FOLLOWING
Chappell accepts the award for Best New Artist at the 2024 MTV Video Music Awards in New York.

Awards and Nominations

Billboard Music Award

2024: Top New Artist (Won)

BreakTudo Awards

2024: International Best New Artist (Nomination)

BRIT Awards

2025: International Artist of the Year (Won)
2025: International Song of the Year for "Good Luck, Babe!" (Won)

Grammy Awards

2025: Best New Artist (Won)
2025: Album of the Year (Nomination)
2025: Record of the Year for "Good Luck, Babe!" (Nomination)
2025: Song of the Year for "Good Luck, Babe!" (Nomination)
2025: Best Pop Solo Performance for "Good Luck, Babe!" (Nomination)
2025: Best Pop Vocal Album for *The Rise and Fall of a Midwest Princess* (Nomination)

iHeartRadio Music Awards

2025: Pop Artist of the Year (Nomination)
2025: Best New Pop Artist (Nomination)
2025: Favorite Surprise Guest (Nomination)
2025: Favorite Tour Tradition for the "HOT TO GO!" dance (Nomination)
2025: Best Lyrics for "Good Luck, Babe!" (Nomination)
2025: Favorite Tour Style for The Midwest Princess Tour (Nomination)

MTV Europe Music Awards

2024: Best Song for "Good Luck, Babe!" (Nomination)
2024: Best New Artist (Nomination)
2024: Best PUSH (Nomination)
2024: Biggest Fans (Nomination)

MTV Video Music Awards

2024: Best New Artist (Won)
2024: PUSH Performance of the Year for "Red Wine Supernova" (Nomination)
2024: Best Trending Video for "HOT TO GO!" (Nomination)
2024: Song of Summer for "Good Luck, Babe!" (Nomination)

Sources

Alter, Rebecca. "What If I Told You the Song of Summer 2021 Is This Stripper's Delight From Summer 2020?" *Vulture*, May 27, 2021. https://www.vulture.com/article/song-recommendation-chappell-roan-pink-pony-club.html

Anbouba, Margaux. "Chappell Roan on Her First-Ever Coachella and the Magic of Makeup," *Vogue*, April 14, 2024. https://www.vogue.com/article/chappell-roan-coachella

Andrade, Sofia. "Chappell Roan doesn't care if she's going to hell," *The Washington Post*, October 14, 2023. https://www.washingtonpost.com/entertainment/music/2023/10/14/chappell-roan-queer-pop/

Aswad, Jem. "Rising Star Chappell Roan Meets Her Moment With Ecstatic New York Show: Concert Review," *Variety*, March 1, 2023. https://variety.com/2023/music/concert-reviews/chappell-roan-ecstatic-new-york-concert-review-1235539906/

Atlantic Records, School Nights EP, 2017.

Azzopardi, Chris. "We Knew Her When: On the Tour Bus with Chappell Roan," *Qburgh*, August 29, 2024. https://qburgh.com/on-the-tour-bus-with-chappell-roan/

Betancourt, Bianca. "A Behind-the-Scenes Look at Chappell Roan's Legendary *SNL* Debut," *Harper's Bazaar*, November 5, 2025. https://www.harpersbazaar.com/culture/art-books-music/a62802471/ramisha-sattar-chappell-roan-snl-interview-2024/

Billboard. "The 2022 Billboard Power List Revealed," January 26, 2022. https://www.billboard.com/business/business-news/billboard-2022-power-list-1235022798/

Boisvert, Lauren. "3 of Chappell Roan's Early Songs That Prove She's Always Been a Talented Queen," *American Songwriter*, November 2, 2024. https://americansongwriter.com/3-of-chappell-roans-early-songs-that-prove-shes-always-been-a-talented-queen/

Brown, August. "Meet Chappell Roan, L.A.'s queer pop superstar in the making," *Los Angeles Times*, August 29, 2023. https://www.latimes.com/entertainment-arts/music/story/2023-08-29/chappell-roan-fall-preview-queer-pop-diva-rise-and-fall-of-a-midwest-princess

Brown, Melissa. "Tennessee passes controversial drag show bill," *Nashville Tennessean*, Feb 23, 2023. https://www.tennessean.com/story/news/politics/2023/02/23/tennessee-drag-bill-to-ban-certain-performances-passes-general-assembly/69935840007/

Bujnosek, Bailey. "The Altar of Chappell," *V Magazine*, March 29, 2023. https://vmagazine.com/article/at-the-altar-of-chappell/

Cai, Delia. "The femininomenonal ascent of Chappell Roan," *The Face*, September 16, 2024. https://theface.com/music/chappell-roan-pop-music-famous-interview-good-luck-babe

Caldwell, Sophie. "What to know about 'brat summer,' the trend taking over pop culture and politics," Today.com, July 23, 2024. https://www.today.com/popculture/music/what-is-brat-summer-charli-xcx-rcna163061

Carr, Mary Kate, Saloni Gajjar, and Emma Keates. "Chappell Roan is the biggest story out of Gov Ball—and possibly of the whole summer," *The AV Club*, June 10, 2024. https://www.avclub.com/chappell-roan-gov-ball-2024-highlights-1851529729

Castro, Reese, host. "Chappell Roan Interview," Austin Underground YouTube, February 5, 2018. http://youtube.com/watch?v=FnDuUzuSVKY

Chappell Roan Official Instagram, https://www.instagram.com/chappellroan/?hl=en

Chappell Roan Official TikTok. "Im done talking about it . . .," TikTok, September 25, 2024. https://www.tiktok.com/@chappellroan/video/7418582700141055278

Chappell Roan YouTube Page, https://www.youtube.com/channel/UCTKTRVaWrythRIGNfZYBp2A

Czemier, Zuzanna. "Exclusive Track & Video Premiere: 'Good Hurt,' Chappell Roan," *Interview*, August 1, 2017. https://www.interviewmagazine.com/music/premiere-good-hurt-chappell-roan#_

Dacity, Ms. "Chappell Roan: The 'Kaleidoscope' Interview," *Daily Trojan*, March 30, 2023. https://dailytrojan.com/2023/03/30/chappell-roan-kaleidoscope/

Daw, Stephen. "Dan Nigro on Chappell Roan's 'Old School Success' & When He Realized She's 'A Superstar,'" *Billboard*, June 28, 2024. https://www.billboard.com/music/pop/dan-nigro-chappell-roan-good-luck-babe-hot-100-interview-1235719249/

Deatherage, Gunnar. "Making a look for @ chappell roan . . .," TikTok, November 2, 2024. https://www.tiktok.com/@gunnardeatherage/video/7432811714271399211

De Wolfe, Danielle. "One To Watch: Chappell Roan | Good Hurt," *One Stop Record Shop*, August 24, 2017. https://onestoprecordshop.co.uk/music/one-to-watch-chappell-roan-good-hurt.html/

Dodson, P. Claire. "Chappell Roan Talks 'Casual' Music Video, Trans Rights, and Creating the Pink Pony Club of Her Dreams," *Teen Vogue*, March 9, 2023. https://www.teenvogue.com/story/chappell-roan-casual-music-video-trans-rights-pink-pony-club-of-dreams-interview

Fast Company, "Chappell Roan and Olivia Rodrigo producer Daniel Nigro on the secret to 'overnight' success," July 2, 2024. https://www.fastcompany.com/91148805/chappell-roan-and-olivia-rodrigo-producer-daniel-nigro-on-the-secret-to-overnight-success

Fell, Nicole. "Chappell Roan Opens Up About Her Mental Health, Love and Onstage Persona: 'Chappell Is a Character,'" *Hollywood Reporter*, November 8, 2024. https://www.hollywoodreporter.com/news/music-news/chappell-roan-grammy-museum-mental-health-love-onstage-persona-1236056354/

Frick, Evelyn, "Jewish Singer Troye Sivan Lowkey Discovered Chappell Roan in 2014," *Hey Alma*, July 2, 2024. https://www.heyalma.com/jewish-singer-troye-sivan-lowkey-discovered-chappell-roan-in-2014/

Fromson, Audrey. "Chappell Roan on Making Pop Music and Giving Back," *Vanity Fair*, September 18, 2023. https://www.vanityfair.com/style/2023/09/chappell-roan-on-making-pop-music-and-giving-back?srsltid=AfmBOoqWq-5W14RVq-UUEHpwUKPzUqoMCmxui4cEARODvDo_J6hoBK74

Goodstein, Joshua. "'Showgirls,' Camp, and the Making of a Queer Cult Classic," *Screen Speck*, July 19, 2022. https://screenspeck.com/2022/07/19/showgirls-camp-and-the-making-of-a-queer-cult-classic/

Headliner, "Chappell Roan: How an Unforgettable Night at a Gay Club Led to Pink Pony Club," circa 2020. https://headlinerhub.com/chappell-roan-california-here-we-come.html

Heart, Mo, host. "Chappell Roan is Bringing TACKY to the Masses (And Why She Loves It)," *The Walk In*, Amazon Music, November 6, 2023. https://www.youtube.com/watch?v=tt-U6vM5bNY

Hoffman, Baylie. "The History of Drag," *Struthers Library Theatre Blog*, June 7, 2023. https://www.strutherslibrarytheatre.org/blog/the-art-and-history-of-drag#:~:text=In%20the%2019th%20century%2C%20drag,and%20hidden%20in%20mainstream%20media.

Holman, Gregory J. "Chappell Roan is a singer from Willard. She just made the big time," *Springfield News-Leader*, August 17, 2017. https://www.news-leader.com/story/entertainment/2017/08/17/chappell-roan-singer-willard-she-just-made-big-time/548315001/

Iowa Public Radio, "Lucy Ritter is taking the pop world by storm as Chappell Roan's drummer," Iowa Public Radio, November 25, 2024. https://www.iowapublicradio.org/studioone/news/2024-11-25/lucy-ritter-is-taking-the-pop-world-by-storm-as-chappell-roans-drummer

Island Records, *The Rise and Fall of a Midwest Princess*, 2023.

Jackson, Hannah. "Genesis Webb Is More Than Chappell Roan's Stylist," *British Vogue*, July 3, 2024. https://www.vogue.co.uk/article/chappell-roan-stylist-genesis-webb

Jeffrey, Joyann, "Who are Chappell Roan's parents? All about her family," Today.com, September 11, 2024. https://www.today.com/parents/celebrity/chappell-roan-parents-rcna170752

Jocelyn, Hannah. "Not Just 'Luck': Why Queer Pop Star Chappell Roan Broke Through to the Hot 100, And Why It Matters," *Billboard*, April 18, 2024. https://www.billboard.com/music/chart-beat/chappell-roan-good-luck-babe-queer-pop-music-1235659813/

John, Elton, host. "Chappell Roan & Elton John: 'Good Luck, Babe,' New Music & Songwriting," *The Rocket Hour*, episode 400, Apple Music, May 25, 2024. https://www.youtube.com/watch?v=UhA_fSGEpYs

Johnston, Maura. "The 10 Best Albums of 2023," *Time*, December 5, 2023. https://time.com/6340131/best-albums-2023/

Kaplan, Ilana. "Chappell Roan on Her Love of Drag Queens and Her Debut Album That 'Feels Like a Party' (Exclusive)," *People*, September 27, 2023. https://people.com/chappell-roan-new-album-rise-fall-midwest-princess-exclusive-7974688

Kleiman, Evan. "How The Abbey overcame adversity to become a West Hollywood institution," KCRW.com, June 23, 2023. https://www.kcrw.com/culture/shows/good-food/abbey-queer-hospitality-pride-month-pies-peaches-sushi/abbey-gay-bar-nightclub-queer-history-david-cooley-west-hollywood

Le, Brendan. "She's Your Favorite Artist's Favorite Artist! 12 Musicians Who Love Chappell Roan, from Beyoncé to Adele," *People*, September 11, 2024. https://people.com/chappell-roan-celebrity-fans-8704362

Levine, Nick. "Chappell Roan: the pop supernova who feels like one of the 'Drag Race' girls," *NME*, February 5, 2024. https://www.nme.com/the-cover/chappell-roan-05-02-2024-3582467

Lewis, Isobel. "Chappell Roan on Elton John, queer stardom, and Olivia Rodrigo's advice," *The Independent*, December 3, 2023. https://www.independent.co.uk/arts-entertainment/music/features/chappell-roan-elton-john-olivia-rodrigo-b2456768.html

Lindsay, Kathryn. "The Drop: Exclusive Music Video Premiere For Chappell Roan's 'Die Young,'" *Refinery29*, January 3, 2018. https://www.refinery29.com/en-us/2018/01/186800/chappell-roan-die-young-music-video

Lisicky, Adam, host. "Interview with Chappell Roan," Bringin' it Backwards YouTube, May 29, 2020. https://www.youtube.com/watch?v=OUELORAMn2c

Lisicky, Adam, host. "Interview with Chappell Roan (Chappell Returns!)," Bringin' it Backwards YouTube, September 13, 2022. https://www.youtube.com/watch?v=TykZd16Cfms

Marks, Craig. "The Rise of Chappell Roan: Behind the Scenes," *Hits Daily Double*, September 13, 2024. https://hitsdailydouble.com/news&id=342414&title=THE-RISE-OF-CHAPPELL-ROAN:-BEHIND-THE-SCENES-

Mier, Tomás. "Chappell Roan's Campy, Glittery Music is the Future of Pop," *Rolling Stone*, March 21, 2024. https://www.rollingstone.com/music/music-features/chappell-roan-pop-lgbtq-olivia-rodrigo-1234981099/

Mitchell, Cece. "Chappell Roan's biggest crowd yet for headlining show in rural Iowa." Iowa Public Radio, October 2, 2024. https://www.iowapublicradio.org/studioone/news/2024-10-04/chappell-roan-iowa-midwest-princess-tour-council-bluffs-snl

Mylrea, Hannah. "Chappell Roan – 'The Rise and Fall Of A Midwest Princess' review: unabashedly fun anthems," *NME*, September 22, 2023. https://www.nme.com/reviews/album/chappell-roan-the-rise-and-fall-of-a-midwest-princess-review-debut-album-radar-3499595

O'Dwyer, Jayne. "Chappell Roan brings unbridled queer emotion to Brooklyn Steel," *Document*, October 24, 2023. https://www.documentjournal.com/2023/10/chappell-roan-the-rise-and-fall-of-a-midwest-princess-tour-review-music/

Olivia's GUTS World Tour. "Olivia Rodrigo & Chappell Roan - HOT TO GO! (Live at The GUTS Tour)" YouTube, October 1, 2024. https://www.youtube.com/watch?v=c68sOUJ6Eb0

Use the QR code to view the full list of sources.

Photo Credits

Page 2: © Kevin Mazur/Getty images

Page 4: © Emilio Madrid/Getty images

Page 6: © Dania Maxwell/Getty images

Page 9: © Imago/Alamy Stock Photo

Page 10: © Kevin Mazur/Getty images

Page 12: © The Washington Post/Getty images

Page 21: © Rodin Eckenroth/Getty images

Page 27: © CBS Photo Archive/Getty images

Page 32: © Astrida Valigorsky/Getty images

Page 36: © Jim Bennett/Getty images

Page 39: © Josh Brasted/Getty images

Page 40: © Dana Jacobs/Getty images

Page 46: © Rebecca Sapp/Getty images

Page 52: © Rebecca Sapp/Getty images

Page 60: © Gilbert Flores/Getty images

Page 64: © John Shearer/Getty images

Page 69: © Rebecca Sapp/Getty images

Page 71: © Stephen J. Cohen/Getty images

Page 75: © Boston Globe/Getty images

Page 80: © Rick Kern/Getty images

Page 82: © Axelle/Bauer-Griffin/Getty images

Page 90: © Rick Kern/Getty images

Page 93: © Rick Kern/Getty images

Page 97: © Pictorial Press Ltd/Alamy Stock Photo

Page 104: © Jason Kempin/Getty images

Page 108: © Jim Dyson/Getty images

Page 118: © Christopher Polk/Getty images

Page 124 © Christopher Polk/Getty images

Page 128: © Jim Dyson/Getty images

Page 134: © ZUMA Press, Inc/Alamy Stock Photo

Page 139: © Kevin Mazur/Getty images

Page 142: © Rebecca Sapp/Getty images

Page 152: © Marleen Moise/Getty images

Page 154: © Dana Jacobs/Getty images

Page 157: © Vivien Killilea/Getty images

Page 158: © Josh Brasted/Getty images

Page 159: © Marleen Moise/Getty images

Page 163: © Katja Ogrin/Getty images

Page 164: © Matt Winkelmeyer/Getty images

Page 170: © Jon Kopaloff/Getty images

Page 172: © Stephen J. Cohen/Getty images

Page 183: © Kevin Mazur/Getty images

Page 188: © The Washington Post/Getty images

Page 190: © Astrida Valigorsky/Getty images

Page 195: © Michael Loccisano/Getty images

Page 196: © The Washington Post/Getty images

Page 199: © Mike Coppola/Getty images

PHOTO CREDITS

Acknowledgments

Thank you to Chappell—of course—for making a world we can all play in. Thanks as well to the crew at Quarto Books, who make it look easy. Finally, special thanks to Mabel for showing me how to H-O-T-T-O-G-O, and to Charles for taking me to Heaven.

About the Author

Harbert Day is the pen name of a bi woman writer who lives in Brooklyn, New York. She left the Midwest when she was twenty years old and still worries about what her mother might think.

© 2025 by Quarto Publishing Group USA Inc.

First published in 2025 by Epic Ink, an imprint of The Quarto Group,
142 West 36th Street, 4th Floor, New York, NY 10018, USA
(212) 779-4972 www.Quarto.com

EEA Representation, WTS Tax d.o.o.,
Žanova ulica 3, 4000 Kranj, Slovenia.
www.wts-tax.si

All rights reserved. No part of this book may be reproduced in any form without written permission of the copyright owners. All images included in this book are original works created by the artist credited on the copyright page, not generated by artificial intelligence, and have been reproduced with the knowledge and prior consent of the artist. The producer, publisher, and printer accept no responsibility for any infringement of copyright or otherwise arising from the contents of this publication. Every effort has been made to ensure that credits accurately comply with the information supplied. We apologize for any inaccuracies that may have occurred and will address inaccurate or missing information in a subsequent reprinting of the book

Epic Ink titles are also available at discount for retail, wholesale, promotional, and bulk purchase. For details, contact the Special Sales Manager by email at specialsales@quarto.com or by mail at The Quarto Group, Attn: Special Sales Manager, 100 Cummings Center Suite 265D, Beverly, MA 01915 USA.

10 9 8 7 6 5 4 3 2 1

ISBN: 978-0-7603-9927-9

Digital edition published in 2025
eISBN: 978-0-7603-9928-6

Library of Congress Control Number: 2025935927

Group Publisher: Rage Kindelsperger
Creative Director: Laura Drew
Managing Editor: Cara Donaldson
Editor: Katelynn Abraham
Cover and Interior Design: Andy Warren Design

Printed in Huizhou, Guangdong, China TT072025

This book has not been prepared, approved, or licensed by the author, producer, or owner of any motion picture, television program, book, game, blog, or other work referred to herein. This is not an official or licensed publication. We recognize further that some words, models' names, and designations mentioned herein are the property of the trademark holder. We use them for identification purposes only.